Practice Tests

for

Andersen/Taylor's

Sociology
The Essentials

Practice Tests

for

Andersen/Taylor's

Sociology
The Essentials

Kathryn Dennick-Brecht
Robert Morris College

WADSWORTH

THOMSON LEARNING

Australia • Canada • Mexico • Singapore • Spain • United Kingdom • United States

For more information, contact
Wadsworth/Thomson Learning
10 Davis Drive
Belmont, CA 94002-3098
USA

For more information about our products, contact us:
Thomson Learning Academic Resource Center
1-800-423-0563
http://www.wadsworth.com

International Headquarters
Thomson Learning
International Division
290 Harbor Drive, 2nd Floor
Stamford, CT 06902-7477
USA

UK/Europe/Middle East/South Africa
Thomson Learning
Berkshire House
168-173 High Holborn
London WC1V 7AA
United Kingdom

Asia
Thomson Learning
60 Albert Complex, #15-01
Singapore 189969

Canada
Nelson Thomson Learning
1120 Birchmount Road
Toronto, Ontario M1K 5G4
Canada

ISBN 0-534-56699-5

Dear Student,

This set of practice tests has been designed as a supplement to the textbook. You can most effectively utilize this book by first carefully reading the textbook and examining each of the instructional guides it contains, including photographs, charts, graphs, and other chapter inserts. After reading the relevant chapter at least once, you can use the material in this book to assist you in identifying concepts which you need to review more carefully. This book contains multiple-choice questions, true-false statements, and short-answer questions for each chapter in the textbook. Further, the correct answers, along with a reference to the appropriate page in the textbook, are provided at the end of each chapter.

I trust that you will find this supplement helpful in assisting you to prepare for your examinations.

Kathy Dennick-Brecht

TABLE OF CONTENTS

Chapter One

SOCIOLOGICAL PERSPECTIVES AND SOCIOLOGICAL RESEARCH

Multiple-Choice Questions. Select the best response.

1. Sociology is:
    a.   the study of human groups from the past
    b.   a scientific way of thinking about society and its influence on human groups
    c.   the only science which provides insight into human behavior
    d.   b and c

2. According to C. Wright Mills, troubles:
    a.   affect large numbers of people, while issues are privately felt problems based on events or emotions in an individual's life
    b.   are the primary focus of sociologists
    c.   are privately felt problems based on an individual's life, while issues affect large numbers of people and are rooted in the institutional arrangements and history of a society
    d.   a and b

3. _____ is (are) the alteration of social interaction, social institutions and society over time.
    a.   Social structure
    b.   Social stability
    c.   The sociological imagination
    d.   Social change

4. Which early sociologist theorized that society is an entity larger than the sum of its parts, that it, society is something to be studied separate from the individuals who compose it?
    a.   Emile Durkheim
    b.   Karl Marx
    c.   Karl Marx
    d.   Alexis deTocqueville

5. Which of the following statements about Jane Addams is FALSE?
    a.   She is the only sociologist to win the Nobel Peace Prize.
    b.   She was a prominent educator who taught at many prestigious universities.
    c.   She was a leader in the settlement house movement, providing community services and conducting systematic research designed to improve the lives of slum dwellers, immigrants, and other dispossessed groups.
    d.   She was a close friend and collaborator with W.E.B. DuBois.

6. Which sociological theory emphasizes the role of coercion and power in producing social order?
    a.   functionalism
    b.   symbolic interaction theory
    c.   conflict theory
    d.   structuralism

7. Which of the following sequences present the correct order for the stages of the research process?
    a.   research question, research design, data collection, data analysis, developing conclusions
    b.   data analysis, research design, research question, data collection, developing conclusions
    c.   research design, data collection, research question, developing conclusions, data analysis
    d.   research question, research design, data analysis, developing conclusions, data collection

8.   A hypothesis is:
      a.   a replication study
      b.   a prediction
      c.   an immigrant
      d.   the dependent variable

9.   In which type of sociological research would a sociologist actually become part of the group that s/he is studying?
      a.   survey research
      b.   prediction
      c.   a controlled experiment
      d.   participant observation

10.   What is debunking?
      a.   the exploration of caves
      b.   a psychological disorder
      c.   looking behind what is taken for granted, that is looking for the origins of social behavior
      d.   the stage of the scientific method in which a researcher collects data

11.   Social institutions are:
      a.   established and organized systems of social behavior with a particular and recognized purpose
      b.   the organized pattern of social relationships that together constitute society
      c.   behaviors between two or more people that are given meaning
      d.   unsettling facts discovered by sociological research

12.   Who believed that the economic organization of society was the most important influence on what humans think and how they behave?
      a.   Emile Durkheim
      b.   Alexis de Tocqueville
      c.   Max Weber
      d.   Karl Marx

13.   What is functionalism?
      a.   a sociological theory emphasizing the role of coercion and power
      b.   a type of architectural design
      c.   a sociological theory which interprets each part of society in terms of how it contributes to the stability of the whole
      d.   the study of past groups to determine their sociological framework

14.   According to sociological research, which of the following statements is (are) true?
      a.   Children raised in single-parent families are less likely than those from two-parent families to hold low-paying jobs in their adult lives.
      b.   Men who work in jobs traditionally defined as "women's work" behave in ways that emphasize their masculinity.
      c.   An African American can expect to earn virtually the same personal income as a White American with the same education, occupation, age and marital status.
      d.   All of the above

15.   Social speedup is characterized by:
      a.   women are more likely to be working outside the house than in previous generations
      b.   less advantaged families need more than one earner to survive
      c.   those who work are working longer hours than previously
      d.   all of the above

16. _____ is defined as the organized pattern of social relationships and social institutions that together constitute society.
    a. Social structure
    b. Symbolic interaction
    c. Functionalism
    d. Government

17. According to Mills, _____ affect large numbers of people and have their origins in the institutional arrangements and history of a society.
    a. troubles
    b. samples
    c. issues
    d. variables

18. Mills thought that to understand the experience of a given person or group of people, one must have knowledge of the social and historical context in which people live. To do this, social scientists must develop:
    a. a sociological imagination
    b. data analysis
    c. objectivity
    d. Social Darwinism

19. The _____ approach to knowledge requires that conclusions be based on careful and systematic observations, rather than previous assumptions.
    a. functional
    b. empirical
    c. conflict
    d. replication

20. Behavior between two or more people that is given meaning is:
    a. social structure
    b. triadic
    c. dyadic
    d. social interaction

21. _____ is the variety of group experiences that result from the social of a society.
    a. Diversity
    b. Social interaction
    c. Cooperation
    d. Social class

22. _____, author of *Democracy in America*, believed that democratic and egalitarian values in the United States influenced American social institutions for the better and transformed personal relationships.
    a. Harriet Martineau
    b. Max Weber
    c. Alexis de Tocqueville
    d. George Herbert Mead

23. The author of the first sociological methods book, *How to Observe manners and Morals*, which discussed how to observe behavior when one is a a participant in the situation being studies, is:
    e. Harriet Martineau
    f. Max Weber
    g. Alexis de Tocqueville
    h. George Herbert Mead

24. _____ refers to understanding social behavior from the point of view of those engaged in it, according to Weber.
    a. Verstehen
    b. Applied sociology
    c. Social Darwinism
    d. Content analysis

25. In Britain, _____ conceived of society as an organism that evolved from simple to complex in a process of adaptation to the environment.
    a. George Herbert Mead
    b. Herbert Spencer
    c. Charles Horton Cooley
    d. Robert Park

26. W.E.B. DuBois:
    a. was a prominent Black scholar and received the first Ph.D. from Harvard which was awarded to a Black person
    b. was a co-founder of the NAACP (National Association for the Advancement of Colored Persons)
    c. argued that "the problem of the twentieth century is the problem of the color line."
    d. all of the above

27. Theoretical frameworks that center on face-to-face social interactions are known as:
    a. verstehen
    b. microsociology
    c. macrosociology
    d. generalizations

28. Which sociological theory interprets each part of society in terms of how it contributes to the stability of the whole?
    a. conflict theory
    b. symbolic interaction theory
    c. functionalism
    d. participant observation

29. According to Robert Merton, _____ are the stated and open goals of social behavior.
    a. manifest functions
    b. variable functions
    c. latent functions
    d. explicit functions

30. Research that is repeated exactly, but on a different group of people or in a different time or place, is called a:
    a. repetitive study
    b. duplication study
    c. replication study
    d. all of the above

31. The _____ is the variable that the researcher wants to test as the presumed cause of something else.
    a. dependent variable
    b. generalization
    c. hypothesis
    d. independent variable

32. A measure is _____ if repeating the measurement gives the same result.
    a. reliable
    b. valid
    c. functional
    d. none of the above

33. A large collection of data, such as national opinion polls, census data, or national crime statistics, is known as a:
    a. data set
    b. data analysis
    c. database
    d. a and c

34. The ability to draw conclusions from specific data and be able to apply them to a broader population is:
    a. replication
    b. generalization
    c. the scientific method
    d. applied sociology

35. When sociologist Judith Rollins posed as a maid and hired herself out in order to collect data, which of the following techniques was she using?
    a. participant observation
    b. controlled experiment
    c. comparative research
    d. evaluation research

36. _____ is a way of learning about a society via investigating such cultural artifacts as newspapers, magazines, or popular music.
    a. Media review
    b. Artifact analysis
    c. Content analysis
    d. Popular culture critique

37. _____ assesses the effects of policies and programs on people in society.
    a. Evaluation research
    b. Comparative research
    c. Historical research
    d. Content analysis

38. A _____ is a relatively large collection of people or other units that a researcher studies and about which generalizations are made.
    a. sample
    b. replication
    c. hypothesis
    d. population

39. Which of the following is (are) true?
    a. Most sociologists do not claim to be value-free, but they try to produce objective research.
    b. Sociological research often raises ethical questions.
    c. Participant observation, if done without the knowledge of people being studied, is a form of deception.
    d. All of the above

40.   The _____ is the presumed effect in a controlled experiment.
   a.   independent variable
   b.   hypothesis
   c.   dependent variable
   d.   replication

True-False Statements.

1.   According to sociological research, relative to girls, boys receive less attention and encouragement in the United States educational system.

2.   Debunking is sometimes easier to do when looking at a culture or society different from one's own.

3.   Since 1970, the gap between Black and White median family income in the United States has narrowed significantly.

4.   By the year 2010, ten percent of the population of the United States under eighteen years old will be members of minority groups.

5.   Lester Ward Frank used Chicago as a living laboratory to study ethnicity, immigration, neighborhood segregation, and urban life.

6.   Theories that strive to understand society as a whole comprise macrosociology.

7.   Latent functions, according to Robert Merton, are the unintended consequences of behavior.

8.   A generalization is a prediction or tentative assumption that a scientists intends to test.

9.   The validity of a measurement is the degree to which it accurately measures or reflects a concept.

10.   Data analysis is the process by which sociologists organize collected data in order to discover the patterns and uniformities that the data reveal.

11.   In the participant observation method of data collection, the sociologist plays two roles at the same time, namely a subjective participant and an objective observer.

12.   A probability is the likelihood that a specific behavior or event will occur.

13.   The subset of a population is the hypothesis.

14.   In comparative research, sociologists examine how features in two or more societies shape social behavior.

15.   A scientific random sample gives everyone in the population an equal chance of being studied.

Short-Answer Questions.
A page reference to the relevant text material is provided in the parenthesis.

1.   Define the concepts of troubles and issues presented by C. Wright Mills (5).

2.   According to Robert Merton, what are manifest and latent functions? Provide at least one example of each (18).

3   According to conflict theory, why does inequality exist? How doe sit continue (26)?

4   List and discuss the five steps in the research process. Is it necessary for these steps to be completed in a particular order? Why or why not (21)?

5.   List and discuss three types of statistical mistakes which might occur in sociological research (25).

ANSWERS TO THE MULTIPLE-CHOICE QUESTIONS.

1.	B	3	Sociology is a scientific way of thinking about society and its influence on human groups.
2.	C	5	According to C. Wright Mills, troubles are privately felt problems based on an individual's life, while issues affect large numbers of people and are rooted in the institutional arrangements and history of a society.
3.	D	9	Social change is the alteration of social interaction, social institutions and society over time.
4.	A	14	Emile Durkheim theorized that society is an entity larger than the sum of its parts, that it, society is something to be studied separate from the individuals who compose it.
5.	B	17	Jane Addams is the only sociologist to win the Nobel Peace Prize. She was a leader in the settlement house movement, providing community services and conducting systematic research designed to improve the lives of slum dwellers, immigrants, and other dispossessed groups. She was a close friend and collaborator with W.E.B. DuBois.
6.	C	18	Conflict theory emphasizes the role of coercion and power in producing social order.
7.	A	21	The correct order for the stages of the research process are: research question, research design, data collection, data analysis, developing conclusions.
8.	B	22	A hypothesis is a prediction.
9.	D	25	In participant observation, a sociologist actually becomes part of the group that s/he is studying.
10.	C	6	Debunking is looking behind what is taken for granted, that is looking for the origins of social behavior.
11.	A	9	Social institutions are established and organized systems of social behavior with a particular and recognized purpose.
12.	D	15	Karl Marx believed that the economic organization of society was the most important influence on what humans think and how they behave.
13.	C	18	Functionalism is the sociological theory which interprets each part of society in terms of how it contributes to the stability of the whole.
14.	B	2	According to sociological research, men who work in jobs traditionally defined as "women's work" behave in ways that emphasize their masculinity.
15.	D	4	Social speedup is characterized by women are more likely to be working outside the house than in previous generations, less advantaged families need more than one earner to survive, and those who work are working longer hours than previously.
16.	A	5	Social structure is defined as the organized pattern of social relationships and social institutions that together constitute society.
17.	C	5	According to Mills, issues affect large numbers of people and have their origins in the institutional arrangements and history of a society.
18.	A	4	Mills thought that to understand the experience of a given person or group of people, one must have knowledge of the social and historical context in which people live. To do this, social scientists must develop a sociological imagination.
19.	B	6	The empirical approach to knowledge requires that conclusions be based on careful and systematic observations, rather than previous assumptions.
20.	D	9	Behavior between two or more people that is given meaning is social interaction.
21.	A	10	Diversity is the variety of group experiences that result from the social of a society.
22.	C	13	Alexis de Tocqueville, author of *Democracy in America*, believed that democratic and egalitarian values in the United States influenced American social institutions for the better and transformed personal relationships.

23.	A	14	The author of the first sociological methods book, *How to Observe manners and Morals*, which discussed how to observe behavior when one is a a participant in the situation being studies, is Harriet Martineau.
24.	A	15	Verstehen refers to understanding social behavior from the point of view of those engaged in it, according to Weber.
25.	B	16	In Britain, Herbert Spencer conceived of society as an organism that evolved from simple to complex in a process of adaptation to the environment.
26.	D	17	W.E.B. DuBois was a prominent Black scholar and received the first Ph.D. from Harvard which was awarded to a Black person, was a co-founder of the NAACP (National Association for the Advancement of Colored Persons), and argued that "the problem of the twentieth century is the problem of the color line."
27.	B	18	Theoretical frameworks that center on face-to-face social interactions are known as microsociology.
28.	C	18	Functionalism interprets each part of society in terms of how it contributes to the stability of the whole.
29.	A	18	According to Robert Merton, manifest functions are the stated and open goals of social behavior.
30.	C	22	Research that is repeated exactly, but on a different group of people or in a different time or place, is called a replication study.
31.	D	23	The independent variable is the variable that the researcher wants to test as the presumed cause of something else.
32.	A	23	A measure is valid if repeating the measurement gives the same result.
33.	D	23	A large collection of data, such as national opinion polls, census data, or national crime statistics, is known as a data set or database.
34.	B	24	The ability to draw conclusions from specific data and be able to apply them to a broader population is generalization.
35.	A	26	When sociologist Judith Rollins posed as a maid and hired herself out in order to collect data, she was using participant observation.
36.	C	26	Content analysis is a way of learning about a society via investigating such cultural artifacts as newspapers, magazines, or popular music.
37.	A	27	Evaluation research assesses the effects of policies and programs on people in society.
38.	D	27	A population is a relatively large collection of people or other units that a researcher studies and about which generalizations are made.
39.	N	28	Most sociologists do not claim to be value-free, but they try to produce objective research. Sociological research often raises ethical questions. Participant observation, if done without the knowledge of people being studied, is a form of deception.
40.	C	23	The dependent variable is the presumed effect in a controlled experiment.

ANSWERS TO THE TRUE-FALSE STATEMENTS.

1.	F	6	According to sociological research, relative to boys, girls receive less attention and encouragement in the United States educational system.
2.	T	7	Debunking is sometimes easier to do when looking at a culture or society different from one's own.
3.	F	7	Since 1970, the gap between Black and White median family income in the United States has remained unchanged.
4.	F	9	By the year 2010, 38 percent of the population of the United States under eighteen years old will be members of minority groups.
5.	F	16	W.I. Thomas and Florian Znaniecki used Chicago as a living laboratory to study ethnicity, immigration, neighborhood segregation, and urban life.
6.	T	17	Theories that strive to understand society as a whole comprise macrosociology.
7.	T	18	Latent functions, according to Robert Merton, are the unintended consequences of behavior.

8.	F	22	A hypothesis is a prediction or tentative assumption that a scientists intends to test.
9.	T	23	The validity of a measurement is the degree to which it accurately measures or reflects a concept.
10.	T	23	Data analysis is the process by which sociologists organize collected data in order to discover the patterns and uniformities that the data reveal.
11.	T	25	In the participant observation method of data collection, the sociologist plays two roles at the same time, namely a subjective participant and an objective observer.
12.	T	27	A probability is the likelihood that a specific behavior or event will occur.
13.	F	27	The subset of a population is the sample.
14.	T	27	In comparative research, sociologists examine how features in two or more societies shape social behavior.
15.	T	28	A scientific random sample gives everyone in the population an equal chance of being studied.

Chapter Two

CULTURE

Multiple-Choice Questions. Select the best response.

1. _____ is the complex system of meaning and behavior that defines the way of life for a given group or society.
    a.   Social structure
    b.   Culture
    c.   Cultural capital
    d.   Cultural hegemony

2. The norms, laws, customs, ideas, and beliefs of a group comprise their:
    a.   nonmaterial culture
    b.   cultural hegemony
    c.   material culture
    d.   social sanctions

3. Which of the following statements about culture is (are) true?
    a.   Culture is learned.
    b.   Culture is stable across time and place.
    c.   Cultural symbols are universal; that is, when an object is defined as a symbol in one culture, it is accepted as a symbol in all cultures.
    d.   All of the above.

4. Things or behaviors to which people give meaning are known as:
    a.   sanctions
    b.   mores
    c.   folkways
    d.   symbols

5. The belief that something can be understood and judged only in relationship to the cultural context in which it appears is:
    a.   ethnocentrism
    b.   cultural diffusion
    c.   cultural relativism
    d.   ethnomethodology

6. According to the Sapir-Whorf hypothesis:
    a.   language determines other aspects of culture
    b.   language determines what people think and perceive
    c.   both of the above
    d.   neither of the above

7. A set of symbols and rules that, put together in a meaningful way, provides a complex communication system is:
    a.   language
    b.   culture
    c.   a dialect
    d.   an argot

8.	An example of a _____ is the custom of men in the United States wearing pants rather than skirts.
	a.	sanction
	b.	law
	c.	more
	d.	folkway

9.	Strict norms that control moral and ethical behavior are:
	a.	sanctions
	b.	laws
	c.	mores
	d.	folkways

10.	_____ is a technique for studying human interaction by deliberately disrupting social norms and observing how individuals respond.
	a.	Crime
	b.	Ethnomethodology
	c.	Deviance
	d.	Ethnocentrism

11.	Shared ideas held collectively by people within a given culture are:
	a.	beliefs
	b.	values
	c.	symbols
	d.	norms

12.	The abstract standards in a society or group that define ideal principles are:
	a.	beliefs
	b.	values
	c.	symbols
	d.	norms

13.	Which of the following statements about dominant cultures is (are) true?
	a.	The dominant culture is the culture of the most powerful group in society.
	b.	A dominant culture is the culture of the majority of people.
	c.	In the United States, sociologists agree that upper-class White males form the dominant culture.
	d.	All of the above

14.	The cultures of groups whose values and norms of behavior are somewhat different from those of the dominant culture are:
	a.	countercultures
	b.	minority cultures
	c.	subgroups
	d.	subcultures

15.	Subcultures created as a reaction against the values of the dominant society are:
	a.	countercultures
	b.	diffuse cultures
	c.	ethnic subcultures
	d.	radical cultures

16. _____ is the habit of seeing things only from the point of view of one's own group.
    a. Cultural relativism
    b. Cultural hegemony
    c. Ethnocentrism
    d. Egoism

17. The beliefs, practices and objects that are part of everyday traditions comprise:
    a. high culture
    b. popular culture
    c. counterculture
    d. subculture

18. Those channels of communication that are available to wide segments of the population, including films, television and the Internet, are:
    a. the public media
    b. the media industry
    c. the "dumbing down" of America
    d. the mass media

19. Which of the following statements about the media is (are) TRUE?
    a. The media have enormous power to shape political opinion and behavior.
    b. Television is a powerful force for transmitting cultural values.
    c. More homes in the U.S. have at least one television than have telephone service.
    d. All of the above.

20. The _____ contends that the mass media reflect the values of the general population.
    a. Sapir-Whorf hypothesis
    b. dominant culture hypothesis
    c. reflection hypothesis
    d. truth

21. _____ is the pervasive and extensive influence of one culture throughout society.
    a. Cultural dominance
    b. Cultural hegemony
    c. The dominant culture
    d. Cultural control

22. Those cultural resources that are socially designated as being worthy and that give advantages to groups that possess them are:
    a. cultural capital
    b. cultural hegemony
    c. cultural values
    d. the dominant value system

23. The new interdisciplinary field of _____, which builds on the insights of the symbolic interaction perspective in sociology, has emerged to study culture.
    a. culturology
    b. psycho-sociology
    c. cultural studies
    d. enthnocentrology

24. The delay in cultural adjustments to changing social conditions is:
    a. cultural lag
    b. cultural diffusion
    c. cultural relativism
    d. cultural resistance

25. Which of the following statements about cultural change is (are) TRUE?
    a. Cultures resist change through cultural diffusion.
    b. Cultural changes are always chosen by the majority of persons in a society.
    c. Cultures change in response to changes in society.
    d. All of the above.

26. The transmission of cultural elements from one society or cultural group to another is known as:
    a. cultural hegemony
    b. cultural diffusion
    c. cultural relativism
    d. cultural capital

27. The pattern of etiquette in the United States, including using a knife, fork, and spoon to eat, is an example of a:
    a. folkway
    b. law
    c. more
    d. belief

28. Strict norms, such as the prohibition against killing humans, which are sometimes supported by laws, are known as:
    a. folkways
    b. values
    c. beliefs
    d. mores

29. In a famous series of experiments, college students were asked to pretend they were boarders in their own homes for a period of fifteen minutes to one hour, without telling their families what they were doing. Which research technique were they using?
    a. controlled experiment
    b. comparative research
    c. ethnomethodology
    d. evaluative research

30. The political conflict over abortion is a conflict over:
    a. values
    b. folkways
    c. symbols
    d. the reflection hypothesis

True-False Statements.

1. Learning the language of a culture is essential to becoming part of a society.

2. Language can reproduce racist and sexist thinking.

3. In response to violations of norms, society often imposes positive sanctions.

4. Values help to bind a culture together, and therefore are always the basis for social cohesion.

14

5.   A dominant culture need not be the culture of the majority of people.

6.   Participation in elite forms of culture is expensive and therefore is shaped by the class status of different groups.

7.   The majority of adults in the U.S. get most of their news from the Internet.

8.   Functionalists believe that contemporary culture is produced within institutions that are based on inequality and capitalist principles.

9.   Even though African Americans and Hispanics watch more television than Whites do, they are a small proportion of TV characters, generally confined to a narrow variety of character types, depicted in stereotyped ways.

10.   Cultural hegemony refers to the cultural resources that are designated as being valuable.

11.   Cultures change as the result of innovation, including technological developments.

12.   Cultural change can be imposed, such as when a powerful group takes over a society and imposes their culture on it.

Short-Answer Questions.
A page reference to the relevant text material is provided in the parenthesis.

1.   List and discuss the characteristics of culture discussed in the textbook (33).

2.   Define and present one example of each of the following types of norms: folkways, mores, and law (39).

3.   Define and discuss each of the following: dominant culture, subculture, and counterculture. Provide one example of each (43).

4.   What are the mass media? How do the media reflect racism and sexism in the United States (50)?

5.   Discuss the four causes of cultural change presented in the textbook. Provide at laest one example of a change caused by each process (55).

ANSWERS TO THE MULTIPLE-CHOICE QUESTIONS

1.	B	32	Culture is the complex system of meaning and behavior that defines the way of life for a given group or society.
2.	A	33	The norms, laws, customs, ideas, and beliefs of a group comprise their nonmaterial culture.
3.	A	33	Culture is learned.
4.	D	34	Things or behaviors to which people give meaning are known as symbols.
5.	C	35	The belief that something can be understood and judged only in relationship to the cultural context in which it appears is cultural relativism.
6.	C	36	According to the Sapir-Whorf hypothesis language determines other aspects of culture and language determines what people think and perceive.
7.	A	36	A set of symbols and rules that, put together in a meaningful way, provides a complex communication system is language.
8.	D	39	An example of a folkway is the custom of men in the United States wearing pants rather than skirts.
9.	C	39	Strict norms that control moral and ethical behavior are mores.
10.	B	39	Ethnomethodology is a technique for studying human interaction by deliberately

disrupting social norms and observing how individuals respond.

11.	A	40	Shared ideas held collectively by people within a given culture are beliefs.
12.	B	40	The abstract standards in a society or group that define ideal principles are values.
13.	A	43	The dominant culture is the culture of the most powerful group in society.
14.	D	43	The cultures of groups whose values and norms of behavior are somewhat different from those of the dominant culture are subcultures.
15.	A	45	Subcultures created as a reaction against the values of the dominant society are countercultures.
16.	C	46	Ethnocentrism is the habit of seeing things only from the point of view of one's own group.
17.	B	48	The beliefs, practices and objects that are part of everyday traditions comprise popular culture.
18.	D	50	Those channels of communication that are available to wide segments of the population, including films, television and the Internet, are the mass media.
19.	D	50	The media have enormous power to shape political opinion and behavior. Television is a powerful force for transmitting cultural values. More homes in the U.S. have at least one television than have telephone service.
20.	C	52	The reflection hypothesis contends that the mass media reflect the values of the general population.
21.	B	54	Cultural hegemony is the pervasive and extensive influence of one culture throughout society.
22.	A	54	Those cultural resources that are socially designated as being worthy and that give advantages to groups that possess them are cultural capital.
23.	C	54	The new interdisciplinary field of cultural studies, which builds on the insights of the symbolic interaction perspective in sociology, has emerged to study culture.
24.	A	55	The delay in cultural adjustments to changing social conditions is cultural lag.
25.	C	55	Cultures change in response to changes in society.
26.	B	55	The transmission of cultural elements from one society or cultural group to another is known as cultural diffusion.
27.	A	39	The pattern of etiquette in the United States, including using a knife, fork, and spoon to eat, is an example of a folkway.
28.	D	39	Strict norms, such as the prohibition against killing humans, which are sometimes supported by laws, are known as mores.
29.	C	39	In a famous series of experiments, college students were asked to pretend they were boarders in their own homes for a period of fifteen minutes to one hour, without telling their families what they were doing. They were using ethnomethodology.
30.	A	40	The political conflict over abortion is a conflict over values.

ANSWERS TO THE TRUE-FALSE STATEMENTS.

1.	T	36	Learning the language of a culture is essential to becoming part of a society.
2.	T	39	Language can reproduce racist and sexist thinking.
3.	F	39	In response to violations of norms, society often imposes negative sanctions.
4.	F	40	Values can be a basis for social cohesion, but they can also be a source of conflict.
5.	T	43	A dominant culture need not be the culture of the majority of people.
6.	T	49	Participation in elite forms of culture is expensive and therefore is shaped by the class status of different groups.
7.	F	50	The majority of adults in the U.S. get most of their news from television.
8.	F	53	Conflict theorists believe that contemporary culture is produced within institutions that are based on inequality and capitalist principles.
9.	T	51	Even though African Americans and Hispanics watch more television than Whites do, they are a small proportion of TV characters, generally confined to a narrow variety of character types, depicted in stereotyped ways.
10.	F	54	Cultural capital refers to the cultural resources that are designated as being valuable.
11.	T	55	Cultures change as the result of innovation, including technological developments.

12.　　T　　56　　Cultural change can be imposed, such as when a powerful group takes over a society and imposes their culture on it.

Chapter Three

SOCIALIZATION

Multiple-Choice Questions. Select the best response.

1. _____ is the term for a few rare people who seem to have been raised in the complete absence of human contact.
    a.   Significant others
    b.   Feral children
    c.   Ego children
    d.   Rock stars

2. The process through which people learn the expectations of society is _____.
    a.   socialization
    b.   the looking-glass self
    c.   resocialization
    d.   social acquisition

3. The expected behavior associated with a given status in society is known as a(n):
    a.   master status
    b.   achieved status
    c.   ascribed status
    d.   role

4. Which of the following statements about socialization is TRUE?
    a.   Socialization creates the capacity for role-taking, or allows us to see ourselves as others see us.
    b.   Socialization creates the tendency for people to act in socially acceptable ways.
    c.   Socialization makes people bearers of culture.
    d.   All of the above.

5. _____ depicts the human psyche as divided into three parts: the id, the superego, and the ego.
    a.   Functionalism
    b.   Object relations theory
    c.   Psychoanalytic theory
    d.   Social learning theory

6. According to Sigmund Freud, the portion of the personality that consists of deep drives and impulses is the:
    a.   superego
    b.   id
    c.   ego
    d.   looking-glass self

7. The key concepts of object relations theory, which refer to the individual's unconscious making and breaking of bonds with parents, are:
    a.   attachment
    b.   resocialization
    c.   individuation
    d.   a and c

8. _____ proposed that children go through distinct stages of cognitive development as they learn the basic rules of reasoning.
   a. George Herbert Mead
   b. Charles Horton Cooley
   c. Jean Piaget
   d. Sigmund Freud

9. The stage at which children begin to use language and other symbols is the:
   a. preoperational stage
   b. concrete operational stage
   c. sensorimotor stage
   d. formal operational stage

10. The concept developed by Charles Horton Cooley to explain how a person's conception of self arises through reflection about relationships to others is the:
    a. looking-glass self
    b. reflection hypothesis
    c. generalized other
    d. resocialization process

11. According to George Herbert Mead, when children begin to take on the roles of significant people in their environment, not just imitating but incorporating their relationship to the other, they are:
    a. in the imitation stage
    b. in the game stage
    c. in the play stage
    d. role-acquisition

12. The passive, conforming self which reacts to others, according to George Herbert Mead, is the:
    a. id
    b. me
    c. I
    d. superego

13. According to sociologists, _____ are those who pass on social expectations.
    a. social etiquette instructors
    b. government officials
    c. cultural transmission agents
    d. socialization agents

14. _____ are those with whom a person interacts on equal terms.
    a. Friends
    b. Co-workers
    c. Peers
    d. Colleagues

15. Which of the following statements about socialization in schools is TRUE?
    a. Research shows that boys receive more attention than girls from teachers.
    b. Teachers are more likely to define middle-class students as trouble-makers than working-class students.
    c. Girls and women are more typically depicted as active players in history, society, and culture than boys and men.
    d. All of the above

16. The informal and often subtle messages about social roles that are conveyed through classroom interaction and classroom materials is the:
    a. subliminal curriculum
    b. hidden curriculum
    c. unofficial curriculum
    d. all of the above

17. Barrie Thorne's research on children suggests which of the following strategies for improving cross-gender and cross-race relationships among children?
    a. Affirm and reinforce the values of cooperation among all children, regardless of social categories.
    b. Whenever possible, organize students into small, heterogeneous, and cooperative work groups.
    c. Actively intervene to challenge the dynamics of stereotyping and power.
    d. All of the above

18. Which of the following are typically considered socialization agents?
    a. religion
    b. peer groups
    c. the media
    d. all of the above

19. Sociologists use the term _____ to describe and analyze the connection between the life events people experience and the sociohistorical context of those events.
    a. life course
    b. life cycle
    c. historical cycle
    d. personal experience

20. _____ involves learning behaviors and attitudes appropriate to specific situations and roles.
    a. Resocialization
    b. Adult socialization
    c. Role socialization
    d. Role acquisition

21. The learning of expectations associated with a role one expects to enter in the future is:
    a. adult socialization
    b. professional development
    c. resocialization
    d. anticipatory socialization

22. _____ are preconceived judgments about what different age groups are like.
    a. Age stereotypes
    b. Age prejudice
    c. Age discrimination
    d. Ageism

23. Which of the following statements about aging is (are) TRUE?
    a. Most old people live in poverty.
    b. Most old people are lonely.
    c. Only 10 percent of old people suffer even a mild loss of memory.
    d. All of the above

24.   The different and unequal treatment of people based solely on their age is:
       a.   age stereotyping
       b.   age discrimination
       c.   ageism
       d.   age prejudice

25.   Sociologists refer to the institutionalized practice of age prejudice and discrimination as:
       a.   ageism
       b.   age stereotyping
       c.   age racism
       d.   age sexism

26.   A(n) _____ is a ceremony or ritual that marks the passage of an individual from one role to another.
       a.   rite of passage
       b.   initiation ceremony
       c.   formal event
       d.   cultural celebration

27.   Sociologists refer to the process by which existing social roles are radically altered or replaced as:
       a.   role reversion
       b.   adult socialization
       c.   anticipatory socialization
       d.   resocialization

28.   The theory which views identity as a learned response to social stimuli as:
       a.   psychoanalysis
       b.   social learning
       c.   symbolic interaction
       d.   object relations

29.   Which of the following statements about Cooley's looking-glass self is (are) TRUE?
       a.   We think about how we appear to others.
       b.   We think about how others judge us.
       c.   We consider how others' perceptions of us make us feel.
       d.   All of the above

30.   According to Piaget, the human mind organizes experiences into mental categories or _____, which are modified and developed as social experiences accumulate.
       a.   captions
       b.   schema
       c.   statuses
       d.   files

True-False Statements.

1.   According to Peter Berger, not only do people live in society, but society also lives in people.

2.   According to psychoanalytic theory, the id is the dimension of the self that represents the standards of society.

3.   Nancy Chodorow's theory argues that a greater valuing of motherhood coupled with greater involvement of men in early child care will produce less gender-stereotyped personalities.

4.   Taking the role of the other is the process of imagining oneself from the point of view of another.

5.   The first agent of socialization for most persons is the school, either at the preschool or elementary level.

6.   Researchers have noted that while many similarities exist, Japanese and United States mothers evidence strong cultural differences in their verbal interactions with their babies.

7.   It is common for individuals to change to a different religious faith than that of their parents.

8.   Research on returning adult women students finds that women who lack the support of family and friends have significant emotional difficulties adjusting to the multiple roles of student, wife, and mother.

9.   Forcible confinement and physical torture can be instruments of extreme resocialization.

10.   Object relations theorists believe that people become who they are through their interactions with others.

11.   Statuses are sets of expectations that govern a person's relationship with people and society.

12.   For most women, playing or watching sports is often the context for developing relationships with mothers, even when the mother is absent or emotionally distant in other areas of life.

Short-answer Questions.
A page reference to the relevant text material is provided in parenthesis.

1.   List and briefly describe the four theoretical perspectives that sociologists use to understand socialization, which were discussed in the textbook (64).

2.   List and discuss the agents of socialization which were discussed in the textbook. Which do you believe is the most important? Why (68)?

3.   Identify four myths about the aged, and discuss why they are incorrect (81).

4.   Discuss the four consequences of socialization which were discussed in the textbook (63).

5.   Discuss each of the three parts of the personality posited by Sigmund Freud. What function is performed by each (64)?

6.   Discuss the stages of cognitive development identified by Jean Piaget (66).

ANSWERS TO THE MULTIPLE-CHOICE QUESTIONS.

1.	60	B	Feral children is the term for a few rare people who seem to have been raised in the complete absence of human contact.
2.	60	A	The process through which people learn the expectations of society is socialization.
3.	60	D	The expected behavior associated with a given status in society is known as a role.
4.	63	D	Socialization creates the capacity for role-taking, or allows us to see ourselves as others see us. Socialization creates the tendency for people to act in socially acceptable ways. Socialization makes people bearers of culture.
5.	64	C	Psychoanalytic theory depicts the human psyche as divided into three parts: the id, the superego, and the ego.
6.	64	B	According to Sigmund Freud, the portion of the personality that consists of deep drives and impulses is the id.
7.	65	D	The key concepts of object relations theory, which refer to the individual's unconscious making and breaking of bonds with parents, are attachment and individuation.
8.	66	C	Jean Piaget proposed that children go through distinct stages of cognitive development as they learn the basic rules of reasoning.
9.	66	A	The stage at which children begin to use language and other symbols is the

preoperational stage.

10. 67 A The concept developed by Charles Horton Cooley to explain how a person's conception of self arises through reflection about relationships to others is the looking-glass self.

11. 68 C According to George Herbert Mead, when children begin to take on the roles of significant people in their environment, not just imitating but incorporating their relationship to the other, they are in the play stage.

12. 68 B The passive, conforming self which reacts to others, according to George Herbert Mead, is the me.

13. 68 D According to sociologists, socialization agents are those who pass on social expectations.

14. 71 C Peers are those with whom a person interacts on equal terms.

15. 74 A Research shows that boys receive more attention than girls from teachers.

16. 74 B The informal and often subtle messages about social roles that are conveyed through classroom interaction and classroom materials is the hidden curriculum.

17. 75 D Barrie Thorne's research on children suggests all of the following strategies for improving cross-gender and cross-race relationships among children. Affirm and reinforce the values of cooperation among all children, regardless of social categories. Whenever possible, organize students into small, heterogeneous, and cooperative work groups. Actively intervene to challenge the dynamics of stereotyping and power.

18. 69 D Religion, peer groups, and the media are typically considered socialization agents.

19. 76 A Sociologists use the term life course to describe and analyze the connection between the life events people experience and the sociohistorical context of those events.

20. 79 B Adult socialization involves learning behaviors and attitudes appropriate to specific situations and roles.

21. 80 D The learning of expectations associated with a role one expects to enter in the future is anticipatory socialization.

22. 81 A Age stereotypes are preconceived judgments about what different age groups are like.

23. 81 C Only 10 percent of old people suffer even a mild loss of memory.

24. 82 B The different and unequal treatment of people based solely on their age is age discrimination.

25. 82 A Sociologists refer to the institutionalized practice of age prejudice and discrimination as ageism.

26. 82 A A rite of passage is a ceremony or ritual that marks the passage of an individual from one role to another.

27. 84 D Sociologists refer to the process by which existing social roles are radically altered or replaced as resocialization.

28. 65 B The theory which views identity as a learned response to social stimuli as social learning theory.

29. 67 D All of the following statements about Cooley's looking-glass self are TRUE. We think about how we appear to others. We think about how others judge us. We consider how others' perceptions of us make us feel.

30. 66 B According to Piaget, the human mind organizes experiences into mental categories or schema, which are modified and developed as social experiences accumulate.

ANSWERS TO TRUE-FALSE STATEMENTS.

1. 62 T According to Peter Berger, not only do people live in society, but society also lives in people.

2. 64 F According to psychoanalytic theory, the superego is the dimension of the self that represents the standards of society.

3. 65 T Nancy Chodorow's theory argues that a greater valuing of motherhood coupled with greater involvement of men in early child care will produce less gender-stereotyped personalities.

4. 67 T Taking the role of the other is the process of imagining oneself from the point of view of another.

5.	69	F	The first agent of socialization for most persons is the family.
6.	69	T	Researchers have noted that while many similarities exist, Japanese and United States mothers evidence strong cultural differences in their verbal interactions with their babies.
7.	71	F	It is rare for individuals to change to a different religious faith than that of their parents.
8.	78	T	Research on returning adult women students finds that women who lack the support of family and friends have significant emotional difficulties adjusting to the multiple roles of student, wife, and mother.
9.	85	T	Forcible confinement and physical torture can be instruments of extreme resocialization.
10.	67	F	Symbolic interactionists believe that people become who they are through their interactions with others.
11.	67	F	Roles are sets of expectations that govern a person's relationship with people and society.
12.	73	F	For most men, playing or watching sports is often the context for developing relationships with fathers, even when the father is absent or emotionally distant in other areas of life.

Chapter Four

SOCIETY AND SOCIAL INTERACTION

Multiple-Choice Questions. Select the best response.

1.   Behavior between two or more people that is meaningful is:
        a.   society
        b.   culture
        c.   social interaction
        d.   proxemic communication

2.   _____ is the term sociologists use to describe the order established in social groups at any level.
        a.   Social interaction
        b.   Social organization
        c.   Social structure
        d.   Impression management

3.   Highly structured social groupings that form to pursue a set of goals are:
        a.   formal organizations
        b.   social categories
        c.   roles
        d.   statuses

4.   Which of the following is a social category?
        a.   Microsoft
        b.   teenagers
        c.   Roman Catholics
        d.   all of the above

5.   An established position in a social structure that carries with it a degree of prestige is a(n):
        a.   role
        b.   nuclear family
        c.   ethnic group
        d.   status

6.   _____ exists when the statuses occupied by an individual bring with them significantly different amounts of prestige.
        a.   Status conflict
        b.   Status inequity
        c.   Status inconsistency
        d.   Status confusion

7.   Most occupational statuses are _____ statuses.
        a.   achieved
        b.   ascribed
        c.   master
        d.   all of the above

8.   A _____ is a collection of expectations that others have for a person occupying a particular status.
   a.   gemeinschaft
   b.   gesellschaft
   c.   role
   d.   social structure

9.   Arlie Hochschild uses which of the following terms to describe the experiences of women who are employed outside of the home?
   a.   neglectful mothers
   b.   working women
   c.   role conflict
   d.   second shift

10.   A condition in which a single role brings conflicting expectations is:
   a.   role conflict
   b.   role strain
   c.   role inconsistency
   d.   gemeninschaft

11.   _____ is a technique for studying human interaction by deliberately disrupting social norms and observing how individuals attempt to restore normalcy.
   a.   Impression management
   b.   Ethnomethodology
   c.   Dramaturgy
   d.   Social exchange

12.   The process by which people control how others perceive them is:
   a.   impression management
   b.   ethnomethodology
   c.   dramaturgy
   d.   social exchange

13.   Goffman's theory, which analyzes social interaction by assuming that the participants are actors on a stage in the nonfiction which is everyday social life, is:
   a.   impression management
   b.   ethnomethodology
   c.   dramaturgy
   d.   social exchange

14.   Which theoretical model of social interaction argues that our interactions are determined by the rewards or punishments that we receive from others?
   a.   collective consciousness
   b.   functionalism
   c.   impression management
   d.   social exchange

15.   When people interact with each other via personal computers, they are engaging in:
   a.   digital discussions
   b.   cyberspace interactions
   c.   proxemic communication
   d.   kinesic communication

16. _____ involves any conveyance of meaning through touch.
   a. Tactile communication
   b. Proxemic communication
   c. Kinesic communication
   d. Paralinguistic communication

17. The component of communication that is conveyed by the pitch and loudness of the speaker's voice, its rhythm, emphasis, and frequency, and the frequency and length of hesitations, is:
   a. tactile communication
   b. proxemic communication
   c. kinesic communication
   d. paralinguistic communication

18. _____ involves gestures, facial expressions, and general body language.
   a. Tactile communication
   b. Proxemic communication
   c. Kinesic communication
   d. Paralinguistic communication

19. Interpersonal attraction is influenced by which of the following?
   a. proximity
   b. perceived physical attractiveness
   c. similarity
   d. all of the above

20. A _____ is an established and organizes system of social behavior with a recognized purpose.
   a. social institution
   b. social category
   c. social structure
   d. division of labor

21. According to functionalist theorists, social institutions perform which of the following functions?
   a. production and distribution of goods and services
   b. socialization of new members of the society
   c. replacement of membership
   d. all of the above

22. Sociologists use the term _____ to refer to the organized pattern of social relationships and social institutions that together compose society.
   a. social interaction
   b. social structure
   c. social organization
   d. culture

23. According to Emile Durkheim, people in a society have a _____, which is a body of beliefs that are common to a community or society and that gives people a sense of belonging and a feeling of moral obligation to its demands and values.
   a. value system
   b. belief structure
   c. collective consciousness
   d. social structure

24. When individuals play a great variety of different roles in a society, so that social unity is based on role differentiation, the society experiences:
    a. mechanical solidarity
    b. a gemeinschaft
    c. role strain
    d. organic solidarity

25. The systematic interrelatedness of different tasks that develops in complex situations is:
    a. division of labor
    b. organic solidarity
    c. resocialization
    d. social organization

26. An industrial society:
    a. typically has a caste system that differentiates the elite from agricultural laborers
    b. typically has an economic system based on the development of elaborate machinery and a factory system
    c. uses gender as the basis for social organization, although division of labor is not rigid and there is little accumulation of wealth
    d. all of the above

27. Information-based societies in which technology plays a vital role in social organization is a(n):
    a. horticultural society
    b. industrial society
    c. pastoral society
    d. postindustrial society

28. Among the rewards which social exchange theorists believe can encourage conforming behavior is (are):
    a. recognition
    b. money
    c. smiles, nods, and pats on the back
    d. all of the above

29. When sociologists try to comprehend the whole of society, including how it is organized and how it changes, they are using which of the following approaches?
    a. microanalysis
    b. ethnomethodology
    c. macroanalysis
    d. impression management

30. The principle of _____ is the idea that our perception of what is real is determined by the subjective meaning that we attribute to an experience.
    a. the social construction of reality
    b. the collective consciousness
    c. proxemic communication
    d. the gemeinschaft

True-False Statements.

1. Persons in a social category interact and communicate with each other, share goals and norms, and have a subjective awareness of themselves as "we."

2. Typically, an individual occupies many statuses simultaneously.

3. According to W. I. Thomas, situations that are defined as real are real in their consequences.

4.   Whenever communication takes place, interaction occurs.

5.   Patterns of tactile communication are strongly influenced by gender.

6.   Men of the same race and culture tend to stand closer to each other in casual conversation than do women of the same race and culture.

7.   Organic solidarity occurs when individuals play similar roles within a society.

8.   A master status may be imposed by others, or a person may define his or her own master status.

9.   The United States is suspended between the industrial and postindustrial phases of economic development.

10. Role strain exists when two or more roles are associated with contradictory expectations.

11. The dramaturgy model of social interaction, developed by Erving Goffman, assumes that participants are actors on the stage in the drama of everyday life.

12. The impression management model of social interaction argues that our interactions are determined by the rewards and punishments that we receive from others.

13. Paralinguistic communication is the component of communication that is conveyed by the pitch and loudness of the speaker's voice, its rhythm, emphasis, and frequency, and the frequency and length of hesitations.

14. Generally, the more friendly a person feels toward another, the closer he or she will stand.

15. Overall, men evidence an affiliative tendency, that is a strong desire to be with other human beings, somewhat more than women.

Short-Answer Questions.
A page reference to the relevant text material is provided in the parenthesis.

1.   Identify the differences between achieved statuses and ascribed statuses. Give three examples of each (91).

2.   Discuss the three characteristics of a group which have been identified by sociologists (90).

3.   Define each of the following terms and provide one example of each: status, status et, status inconsistency, achieved status, ascribed status, and master status (90).

4.   Compare and contrast the following theories of social interaction: the social construction of reality, ethnomethodology, impression management and dramaturgy, and social exchange (93).

5.   Discuss each of the following components of nonverbal communication: tactile communication, paralinguistic communication, kinesic communication, and proxemic communication (99).

ANSWERS TO MULTIPLE-CHOICE QUESTIONS

1.	89	C	Behavior between two or more people that is meaningful is social interaction.
2.	90	B	Social organization is the term sociologists use to describe the order established in social groups at any level.
3.	90	A	Highly structured social groupings that form to pursue a set of goals are formal

			organizations.
4.	90	B	Teenagers are a social category.
5.	90	D	An established position in a social structure that carries with it a degree of prestige is a status.
6.	91	C	Status inconsistency exists when the statuses occupied by an individual bring with them significantly different amounts of prestige.
7.	91	A	Most occupational statuses are achieved statuses.
8.	92	C	A role is a collection of expectations that others have for a person occupying a particular status.
9.	92	D	Arlie Hochschild uses the term second shift to describe the experiences of women who are employed outside of the home.
10.	93	B	A condition in which a single role brings conflicting expectations is role strain.
11.	94	B	Ethnomethodology is a technique for studying human interaction by deliberately disrupting social norms and observing how individuals attempt to restore normalcy.
12.	95	A	The process by which people control how others perceive them is impression management.
13.	95	C	Goffman's theory, which analyzes social interaction by assuming that the participants are actors on a stage in the nonfiction which is everyday social life, is dramaturgy.
14.	97	D	The social exchange model of social interaction argues that our interactions are determined by the rewards or punishments that we receive from others.
15.	97	B	When people interact with each other via personal computers, they are engaging cyberspace interactions.
16.	99	A	Tactile communication involves any conveyance of meaning through touch.
17.	100	D	The component of communication that is conveyed by the pitch and loudness of the speaker's voice, its rhythm, emphasis, and frequency, and the frequency and length of hesitations, is paralinguistic communication.
18.	101	C	Kinesic communication involves gestures, facial expressions, and general body language.
19.	104	D	Interpersonal attraction is influenced by proximity, perceived physical attractiveness, and similarity.
20.	105	A	A social institution is an established and organizes system of social behavior with a recognized purpose.
21.	106	D	According to functionalist theorists, social institutions perform many functions, including the production and distribution of goods and services, socialization of new members of the society, and replacement of membership.
22.	107	B	Sociologists use the term social structure to refer to the organized pattern of social relationships and social institutions that together compose society.
23.	107	C	According to Emile Durkheim, people in a society have a collective consciousness, which is a body of beliefs that are common to a community or society and that gives people a sense of belonging and a feeling of moral obligation to its demands and values.
24.	108	D	When individuals play a great variety of different roles in a society, so that social unity is based on role differentiation, the society experiences organic solidarity.
25.	108	A	The systematic interrelatedness of different tasks that develops in complex situations is division of labor.
26.	110	B	An industrial society typically has an economic system based on the development of elaborate machinery and a factory system.
27.	110	D	Information-based societies in which technology plays a vital role in social organization is a postindustrial society.
28.	97	D	Among the rewards which social exchange theorists believe can encourage conforming behavior are recognition, money, and smiles, nods, and pats on the back.
29.	89	C	When sociologists try to comprehend the whole of society, including how it is organized and how it changes, they are using macroanalysis.
30.	93	A	The principle of the social construction of reality is the idea that our perception of what is real is determined by the subjective meaning that we attribute to an experience.

ANSWERS TO TRUE-FALSE STATEMENTS.

1. 90   F   Persons in a group interact and communicate with each other, share goals and norms, and have a subjective awareness of themselves as "we."
2. 90   T   Typically, an individual occupies many statuses simultaneously.
3. 94   T   According to W. I. Thomas, situations that are defined as real are real in their consequences.
4. 99   F   Some communications are one-way, such as television commercials, and usually involve no communication from the other party.
5. 99   T   Patterns of tactile communication are strongly influenced by gender.
6. 102   F   Women of the same race and culture tend to stand closer to each other in casual conversation than do men of the same race and culture.
7. 107   F   Mechanical solidarity occurs when individuals play similar roles within a society.
8. 91   T   A master status may be imposed by others, or a person may define his or her own master status.
9. 112   T   The United States is suspended between the industrial and postindustrial phases of economic development.
10. 92   F   Role conflict exists when two or more roles are associated with contradictory expectations.
11. 96   T   The dramaturgy model of social interaction, developed by Erving Goffman, assumes that participants are actors on the stage in the drama of everyday life.
12. 97   F   The social exchange model of social interaction argues that our interactions are determined by the rewards and punishments that we receive from others.
13. 100   T   Paralinguistic communication is the component of communication that is conveyed by the pitch and loudness of the speaker's voice, its rhythm, emphasis, and frequency, and the frequency and length of hesitations.
14. 102   T   Generally, the more friendly a person feels toward another, the closer he or she will stand.
15. 103   F   Overall, women evidence an affiliative tendency, that is a strong desire to be with other human beings, somewhat more than men.

Chapter Five

GROUPS AND ORGANIZATIONS

Multiple-Choice Questions. Select the best response.

1.   A group:
       a.   is a collection of individuals who interact with one another
       b.   shares goals and norms
       c.   has a subjective awareness as "we"
       d.   all of the above

2.   _____, according to Simmel, is the tendency for triads to split into a pair and an isolate.
       a.   Triadic division
       b.   Triadic segregation
       c.   Triadic separation
       d.   None of the above. There is no such tendency.

3.   A group consisting of intimate, face-to-face interaction and relatively long-lasting relationships,
       according to Cooley, is a:
       a.   primary group
       b.   secondary group
       c.   triadic group
       d.   dyadic group

4.   Secondary groups are structured to make such goals as making a profit, winning athletic competitions,
       etc. These "task-oriented" needs are also referred to as:
              a.   expressive
              b.   socioemotional
              c.   dyadic
              d.   instrumental

5.   _____ are those to which you may or may not belong, but that you use as a standard for
       evaluating your values, attitudes, and behaviors.
       a.   Primary groups
       b.   Secondary groups
       c.   Reference groups
       d.   Total institutions

6.   The principle that dispositional attributions are made about others under certain conditions, such as out-
       group membership, is:
       a.   attribution theory
       b.   symbolic interaction theory
       c.   status generalization
       d.   functionalist theory

7.   According to attribution theory, which of the following statements is TRUE?
       a.   Observing improper behavior by in-group members, onlookers are likely to attribute the
              deviance to the disposition of the wrongdoer.
       b.   If an in-group member is seen to perform in some laudable way, the behavior is often attributed
              to a variety of special circumstances.
       c.   If an in-group member is seen to perform in some laudable way, the individual is given credit for
              a worthy disposition.
       d.   a and b

8. A set of links between individuals or between other social units, such as bureaucratic organizations or even entire nations, is a:
    a. social structure
    b. social network
    c. social organization
    d. social grouping

9. A branch of research termed _____ studies examines the dynamics of when and how people come to the aid of someone in trouble.
    a. bystander intervention
    b. stranger assistance
    c. nonacquaintance involvement
    d. victim assistance

10. _____ is the term used when the status hierarchy in a society has a measurable effect on behavior within a closed group.
    a. The status effect
    b. The status factor
    c. Status consequences
    d. Status generalization

11. The tendency for group members to reach a consensus opinion, even if that decision is incorrect, is:
    a. group cooperation
    b. groupthink
    c. group flexibility
    d. consensus-building

12. The tendency for groups to weigh risk differently than individuals is:
    a. groupthink
    b. group risk assessment
    c. risky shift
    d. shared responsibility

13. A _____ is a large, secondary group, which is highly organized to accomplish a complex task or tasks and to achieve goals in an efficient manner.
    a. formal organization
    b. primary group
    c. reference group
    d. deindividuated group

14. Which of the following is (are) characteristics of groupthink?
    a. an illusion of unanimity
    b. discouragement of dissenting opinion
    c. an illusion of invulnerability
    d. all of the above

15. Organizations:
    a. tend to be persistent.
    b. can be tools for innovation.
    c. develop cultures and routinized practices.
    d. all of the above.

16. _____, many of which are service or charitable organizations, include the PTA and the NAACP.
   a.   Coercive organizations
   b.   Voluntary organizations
   c.   Utilitarian organizations
   d.   Bureaucracies

17. Membership in a(n) _____ organization is largely involuntary.
   a.   coercive
   b.   voluntary
   c.   utilitarian
   d.   secondary

18. A(n) _____ is an organization cut off from the rest of society and in which the residents are subject to strict social control.
   a.   parochial schools
   b.   bureaucracies
   c.   utilitarian organizations
   d.   total institutions

19. Large organizations, either for profit (such as General Motors) or nonprofit (such as colleges and universities), that are joined by individuals for specific purposes, such as monetary rewards, are:
   a.   coercive
   b.   voluntary
   c.   utilitarian
   d.   total institutions

20. A _____ is a formal organization characterized by an authority hierarchy, a clear division of labor, explicit rules, and impersonality.
   a.   bureaucracy
   b.   coercive organization
   c.   utilitarian organization
   d.   voluntary organization

21. Social interactions in bureaucratic settings that ignore, change, or otherwise bypass the formal structure and rules of the organization are:
   a.   the groupthink structure
   b.   bureaucracy's other face
   c.   triadic segregation
   d.   the formalized bureaucracy

22. _____ has occurred if someone of a higher status within an organization makes unwanted sexual overtures, verbal or nonverbal, toward someone in a relatively lower status position.
   a.   Gender assault
   b.   Sexual teasing
   c.   Sexual harassment
   d.   Gender prejudice

23. Which of the following are problems of bureaucracies in the United States?
   a.   risky shift in work groups
   b.   groupthink
   c.   organizational ritualism
   d.   all of the above

34

24. The explosion of the space shuttle *Challenger* in 1986 was a result of which of the following?
    a. organizational ritualism
    b. groupthink
    c. risky shift
    d. sabotage

25. At times, individuals may become psychologically separated from an organization and its goals. This state of isolation is:
    a. psychosis
    b. neurosis
    c. alienation
    d. a personality disorder

26. A bureaucracy is characterized by:
    a. career ladders
    b. efficiency
    c. impersonal relationships
    d. all of the above

27. Efficiency, calculability, predictability, and control are characteristics of what George Ritzer has termed the:
    a. Disney-effect of bureaucratic structure
    b. McDonaldization of society
    c. blandification of America
    d. standardization of America

28. The organizational theory which postulates that people naturally hate their jobs and want to avoid working and responsibility is:
    a. Theory Y
    b. Theory Z
    c. Theory X
    d. accurate for workers in the United States

29. The organizational form which values long-term employment, interpersonal trust, and above all, close personal relations, is:
    a. Theory Y
    b. Theory Z
    c. Theory X
    d. naïve

30. Quality circles, in which small groups of workers meet periodically with managers to discuss ways the organization can work better, are associated with organizations that use the _____ style of management.
    a. adversarial
    b. Theory Y
    c. Theory Z
    d. competitive

True-False Statements.

1. According to sociological research, jurors are less likely to defect from large factions than from small ones. The larger the faction, the less willing a juror will be to defy the weight of group opinion.

2. Research has shown that identification with reference groups can have a strong effect on self-evaluation and self-esteem.

3. Individuals commonly generate a significantly distorted perception of the motives and capabilities of other people's acts based on whether that person is an in-group or out-group member.

4. A study of White national leaders showed that White leaders form a very closely knit network, which is considerably more dense than that of Black leadership.

5. A large number of studies show that in a situation where a person on the street is in danger, the fewer bystanders there are observing the episode, the less likely anyone will call for the police or an ambulance.

6. There are significant gender differences in patterns of conformity.

7. One explanation of risky shift is that deindividuation occurs, which is the sense that one's self has merged with the group.

8. Organizations develop cultures and routinized practices, which may be reflected in symbols, values, and rituals.

9. People join coercive organizations to pursue goals that they consider personally worthwhile.

10. The informal culture of bureaucracies can become exclusionary and increase the isolation that some workers feel at work.

11. Alienation can be widespread in organizations where manual workers have little control over what they do, but it is not a characteristic of managers.

12. McDonaldization brings many benefits, such as instantaneous service, standardization of pricing and uniform quality of goods, and greater availability of goods and services to a wide proportion of the population.

13. Current pressures on U.S. businesses to enhance profitability through mergers, downsizing, and speedup in productivity have evolved through application of Japanese styles of management to the United States.

14. Traditionally, within organizations, the most powerful positions are held by White men of upper social class status.

15. The conflict perspective argues that the hierarchical or stratified nature of bureaucracies encourages conflict among individuals within them.

Short-Answers Questions.
A page reference to the relevant text material is provided in the parenthesis.

1. Define and discuss each of the following terms: group, dyad, triad, primary group, secondary group, reference group, in-groups and out-groups (116).

2. List and provide one example of each of the four dimensions of attribution errors which tend to favor in-groups over out-groups (119).

3. List and discuss the four characteristics of groupthink which were identified by Janus (126).

4. Define and provide at least one example of each of the following: normative organizations, coercive organizations, utilitarian organizations, and bureaucracies (127).

5. List and discuss the four characteristics of McDonaldization identified by Ritzer (132).

36

6. Identify the principal characteristics of each of the three principal organizational forms discussed in the textbook. Which one do you believe would be most effective in helping the organization to reach its goals? Why (134)?

ANSWERS TO THE MULTIPLE-CHOICE QUESTIONS.

1. D 117 A group is a collection of individuals who interact with one another, shares goals and norms, and has a subjective awareness as "we."

2. B 117 Triadic segregation, according to Simmel, is the tendency for triads to split into a pair and an isolate.

3. A 118 A group consisting of intimate, face-to-face interaction and relatively long-lasting relationships, according to Cooley, is a primary group.

4. D 118 Secondary groups are structured to make such goals as making a profit, winning athletic competitions, etc. These "task-oriented" needs are also referred to as instrumental.

5. C 119 Reference groups are those to which you may or may not belong, but that you use as a standard for evaluating your values, attitudes, and behaviors.

6. A 119 The principle that dispositional attributions are made about others under certain conditions, such as out-group membership, is attribution theory.

7. C 120 If an in-group member is seen to perform in some laudable way, the individual is given credit for a worthy disposition.

8. B 121 A set of links between individuals or between other social units, such as bureaucratic organizations or even entire nations, is a social network.

9. A 122 A branch of research termed bystander intervention studies examines the dynamics of when and how people come to the aid of someone in trouble.

10. D 123 Status generalization is the term used when the status hierarchy in a society has a measurable effect on behavior within a closed group.

11. B 125 The tendency for group members to reach a consensus opinion, even if that decision is incorrect, is groupthink.

12. C 126 The tendency for groups to weigh risk differently than individuals is risky shift.

13. A 127 A formal organization is a large, secondary group, which is highly organized to accomplish a complex task or tasks and to achieve goals in an efficient manner.

14. D 126 The characteristics of groupthink include an illusion of unanimity, discouragement of dissenting opinion, and an illusion of invulnerability.

15. D 127 Organizations tend to be persistent, can be tools for innovation, and develop cultures and routinized practices.

16. B 127 Voluntary organizations, many of which are service or charitable organizations, include the PTA and the NAACP.

17. A 128 Membership in a coercive organization is largely involuntary.

18. D 129 A total institution is an organization cut off from the rest of society and in which the residents are subject to strict social control.

19. C 129 Large organizations, either for profit (such as General Motors) or nonprofit (such as colleges and universities), that are joined by individuals for specific purposes, such as monetary rewards, are utilitarian.

20. A 129 A bureaucracy is a formal organization characterized by an authority hierarchy, a clear division of labor, explicit rules, and impersonality.

21. B 130 Social interactions in bureaucratic settings that ignore, change, or otherwise bypass the formal structure and rules of the organization are bureaucracy's other face.

22. C 130 Sexual harassment has occurred if someone of a higher status within an organization makes unwanted sexual overtures, verbal or nonverbal, toward someone in a relatively lower status position.

23. D 131 Problems of bureaucracies in the United States include risky shift in work groups, groupthink, and organizational ritualism.

24. A 131 The explosion of the space shuttle *Challenger* in 1986 was a result of organizational ritualism.

25. C 132 At times, individuals may become psychologically separated from an organization and

26.	D	129	A bureaucracy is characterized by career ladders, efficiency, and impersonal relationships.
27.	B	132	Efficiency, calculability, predictability, and control are characteristics of what George Ritzer has termed the McDonaldization of society.
28.	C	134	The organizational theory which postulates that people naturally hate their jobs and want to avoid working and responsibility is Theory X.
29.	B	134	The organizational form which values long-term employment, interpersonal trust, and above all, close personal relations, is Theory Z.
30.	C	135	Quality circles, in which small groups of workers meet periodically with managers to discuss ways the organization can work better, are associated with organizations that use the Theory Z style of management.

ANSWERS TO TRUE-FALSE STATEMENTS.

1.	T	116	According to sociological research, jurors are less likely to defect from large factions than from small ones. The larger the faction, the less willing a juror will be to defy the weight of group opinion.
2.	T	119	Research has shown that identification with reference groups can have a strong effect on self-evaluation and self-esteem.
3.	T	119	Individuals commonly generate a significantly distorted perception of the motives and capabilities of other people's acts based on whether that person is an in-group or out-group member.
4.	F	122	A study of Black national leaders showed that Black leaders form a very closely knit network, which is considerably more dense than that of White leadership.
5.	F	122	A large number of studies show that in a situation where a person on the street is in danger, the more bystanders there are observing the episode, the less likely anyone will call for the police or an ambulance.
6.	F	123	There is little gender difference in patterns of conformity.
7.	T	127	One explanation of risky shift is that deindividuation occurs, which is the sense that one's self has merged with the group.
8.	T	127	Organizations develop cultures and routinized practices, which may be reflected in symbols, values, and rituals.
9.	F	127	People join normative organizations to pursue goals that they consider personally worthwhile.
10.	T	130	The informal culture of bureaucracies can become exclusionary and increase the isolation that some workers feel at work.
11.	F	132	Alienation can be widespread in organizations where manual workers have little control over what they do, but it is not restricted to manual laborers.
12.	T	133	McDonaldization brings many benefits, such as instantaneous service, standardization of pricing and uniform quality of goods, and greater availability of goods and services to a wide proportion of the population.
13.	F	134	Current pressures on U.S. businesses to enhance profitability through mergers, downsizing, and speedup in productivity militate against the styles of management associated with Japanese culture.
14.	T	135	Traditionally, within organizations, the most powerful positions are held by White men of upper social class status.
15.	T	137	The conflict perspective argues that the hierarchical or stratified nature of bureaucracies encourages conflict among individuals within them.

Chapter Six

DEVIANCE

Multiple-Choice Questions. Select the best response.

1.   Behavior that is recognized as violating expected rules and norms is:
      a.   violence
      b.   deviance
      c.   crime
      d.   all of the above

2.   Which of the following statements about deviance is (are) TRUE?
      a.   The definition of deviance remains constant over time.
      b.   The definition of deviance remains constant across different societies.
      c.   Deviance may be formal or informal.
      d.   All of the above

3.   Sociologists use the term _____ to refer to explanations of deviant behavior that interpret deviance as the result of individual pathology or sickness.
      a.   medicalization of deviance
      b.   structural strain theory
      c.   labeling theory
      d.   social control theory

4.   According to functionalist theorists, deviance is functional because it:
      a.   is necessary to clarify social norms
      b.   creates social cohesion
      c.   allows the collective identity of a group to be affirmed when those who are defined as deviant are ridiculed or condemned
      d.   all of the above

5.   Why was Durkheim's study of suicide important?
      a.   It criticized the usual psychological interpretations of why people commit suicide.
      b.   It emphasized the role of social structure in producing deviance.
      c.   It identified the importance of individuals' social attachments to society in understanding deviance.
      d.   All of the above

6.   According to Durkheim, _____ is the condition that exists when social regulations in a society break down.
      a.   altruism
      b.   anomie
      c.   egoism
      d.   de-structuralism

7.   Suicide which occurs when people feel totally detached from society is:
      a.   egoistic
      b.   altruistic
      c.   anomic
      d.   integrative

8. Merton's theory, which traces the origins of deviance to the tensions caused by the gap between cultural goals and the means people have to achieve these goals, is termed:
    a. social control theory
    b. labeling theory
    c. structural strain theory
    d. differential association theory

9. According to Travis Hirschi, deviance occurs when a person's or group's attachment to social bonds is weakened. This theory is known as:
    a. social control theory
    b. attachment theory
    c. detachment theory
    d. structural strain theory

10. Which of the following statements about functionalism is (are) TRUE?
    a. Functionalists emphasize that individual motivation produces deviance, rather than social structure.
    b. Critics of functionalism argue that the theory largely ignores the positive effects on society which deviance often contributes.
    c. Functionalism does little to explain why some behaviors are defined as normative and others as legitimate.
    d. All of the above

11. _____ posits that the economic organization of capitalist societies produces deviance and crime.
    a. Differential association theory
    b. Labeling theory
    c. Structural strain theory
    d. Conflict theory

12. The wrongdoing of wealthy and powerful individuals and organizations is:
    a. elite deviance
    b. differential association
    c. corporate deviance
    d. a and c

13. Macrosociological theories of deviance include:
    a. symbolic interaction theory
    b. conflict theory
    c. differential association theory
    d. all of the above

14. _____ theory interprets deviance, including criminal behavior, as behavior one learns through interaction with others.
    a. Social control agent
    b. Labeling
    c. Differential association
    d. Functionalist

15. The definition a person has of himself or herself as a deviant is their:
    a. deviant identity
    b. deviant career
    c. self-concept
    d. deviant label

40

16. Elite deviance includes:
    a. illegal arrangements made for corporate profit
    b. illegal campaign contributions
    c. government actions that abuse public trust, such as secret arms deals or lying about covert activity
    d. all of the above

17. A _____ is the sequence of movements a person makes through different positions in an occupational system.
    a. deviant identity
    b. deviant hierarchy
    c. deviant career
    d. deviant lifestyle

18. Groups that are organized around particular forms of social deviance are:
    a. deviant communities
    b. corporations
    c. gangs
    d. all of the above

19. Which of the following statements about labeling theorists' perspectives on the official statistics on deviance is (are) TRUE?
    a. Labeling theorists argue that official statistics reflect social judgments, not necessarily the actual commission of crimes or deviant acts.
    b. Labeling theorists are more likely to ask how behavior becomes labeled deviant than they are to ask what motivates people to become deviant.
    c. Labeling theorists believe that official rape rates are underestimates of the actual extent of rape.
    d. All of the above

20. Which of the following statements about mental illness is (are) TRUE?
    a. Those people with the fewest resources are most likely to be labeled mentally ill.
    b. Men have higher rates of mental illness than women in the United States.
    c. Women with the most stereotypical female identities, namely passive, dependent, and subservient, are the least likely to suffer from dissatisfaction, anxiety, and low self-esteem.
    d. All of the above

21. A(n) _____ is an attribute that is socially devalued and discredited.
    a. character defect
    b. stigma
    c. personality flaw
    d. egoistic tendency

22. Which of the following crimes is (are) included in the *Uniform Crime Report*?
    a. prostitution
    b. white-collar crimes
    c. larceny
    d. all of the above

23. Illicit activities, such as gambling, illegal drug use and prostitution, in which there is no complainant, are:
    a. victimless crimes
    b. decriminalized offenses
    c. white-collar crimes
    d. organizational deviance

24. Crime which is committed by organized groups and typically involves the provision of illegal goods and services to others is _____ crime.
    a. organizational
    b. white-collar
    c. property
    d. organized

25. Which of the following statements about white-collar crime is (are) TRUE?
    a. White-collar crime is wrongdoing that occurs within the context of a formal organization and is sanctioned by the norms and operating principles of the organization.
    b. Individuals within the organization may participate in white-collar crime with little awareness that their behavior is illegitimate.
    c. White-collar crime seldom generates great concern in the public mind.
    d. All of the above

26. Which of the following statements about law enforcement is (are) TRUE?
    a. Police discretion is greatest when dealing with minor offenses, such as disorderly conduct.
    b. Police discretion is strongly influenced by class and race judgments.
    c. Minority communities are policed much more intensively than White communities, which leads to more frequent arrests for those who live in minority communities.
    d. All of the above

27. Conflict theories of deviance, based on the work of _____, use the macrosociological approach, since they examine the structure of society as a whole in their explanation of deviance.
    a. Emile Durkheim
    b. Karl Marx
    c. Edwin Sutherland
    d. W. I. Thomas

28. _____ is (are) those who regulate(s) and administer(s) the societal response to deviance, such as the police and mental health workers.
    a. Social control agents
    b. The power elite
    c. The upper class
    d. The criminal justice system

29. *The Uniform Crime Report* is published annually in the United States by the:
    a. American Sociological Association
    b. American Association of Criminologists
    c. Federal Bureau of Investigation
    d. It is co-published by all three of these groups.

30. _____ are assaults and other malicious acts directed against gay men, lesbian women, people with disabilities, and racial minorities.
    a. Crimes of prejudice
    b. Crimes of discrimination
    c. White-collar crimes
    d. Hate crimes

True-False Statements.

1. Durkheim argued that societies need deviance in order to understand what normal behavior is.

2. Sociologists criticize the medicalization of deviance for ignoring the effects of social structures on the development of deviant behavior.

42

3. Durkheim's investigation of suicide identified the critical importance of psychological factors as causes of deviant behavior.

4. Sociologists have linked the condition of anomie to a variety of social problems, including juvenile delinquency.

5. According to the social control theory, a prostitute has accepted the cultural values of the dominant society, since s/he wishes to be economically successful and accepts the commercialization of sexuality that characterizes the dominant culture.

6. Conflict theorists argue that members of the upper class can better hide crimes because they have the resources to mask their deviance and crimes.

7. A disability may become the master status for a disabled person. Through this process, the disability overrides all other features of the person's identity.

8. Deviance is one form of crime.

9. Enforcement of victimless crimes is typically more vigorous than the enforcement of crimes against persons or property, since the criminal justice system recognizes the direct correlation between these crimes and violent crimes.

10. Certain groups are more likely to commit crime than others, because crime is distinctively linked to patterns of inequality in society.

11. Racial minority groups are far more likely than Whites to be poor, unemployed, and living in single-parent families and these social factors are predictors of a higher rate of crime.

12. Women's participation in crime has been increasing in recent years.

13. Women are more likely to be victimized by crime than men, although victimization by crime among women varies significantly by race and age.

14. Women's fear of crime increases with age, although the likelihood of victimization decreases with age.

15. In general, prisons seem neither to deter crime nor rehabilitate criminals.

Short-Answer Questions.
A page reference to the relevant text material is provided in the parenthesis.

1. List and describe the three types of suicide which were identified by Emile Durkheim (148).

2. Briefly summarize each of the following theories: structural strain, social control, conflict, differential association, and labeling (147).

3. Discuss the problems with official statistics about deviance which have been identified by labeling theorists. What recommendations could you propose to reduce these problems (155)?

4. What is a stigma and what effect does it have on deviant behavior (157)?

5. Define, discuss, and provide one example of each of the following types of crimes: personal, property, white-collar and organized. What is organizational deviance and how are these offenders punished (158)?

ANSWERS TO THE MULTIPLE-CHOICE QUESTIONS.

1.	B	143	Behavior that is recognized as violating expected rules and norms is deviance.
2.	C	143	Deviance may be formal or informal.
3.	A	146	Sociologists use the term medicalization of deviance to refer to explanations of deviant behavior that interpret deviance as the result of individual pathology or sickness.
4.	D	147	According to functionalist theorists, deviance is functional because it is necessary to clarify social norms, creates social cohesion, and allows the collective identity of a group to be affirmed when those who are defined as deviant are ridiculed or condemned.
5.	D	147	Durkheim's study of suicide was important because it criticized the usual psychological interpretations of why people commit suicide, emphasized the role of social structure in producing deviance, and identified the importance of individuals' social attachments to society in understanding deviance.
6.	B	148	According to Durkheim, anomie is the condition that exists when social regulations in a society break down.
7.	A	148	Suicide which occurs when people feel totally detached from society is egoistic.
8.	C	149	Merton's theory, which traces the origins of deviance to the tensions caused by the gap between cultural goals and the means people have to achieve these goals, is termed structural strain theory.
9.	A	149	According to Travis Hirschi, deviance occurs when a person's or group's attachment to social bonds is weakened. This theory is known as social control theory.
10.	C	150	Functionalism does little to explain why some behaviors are defined as normative and others as legitimate.
11.	D	151	Conflict theory posits that the economic organization of capitalist societies produces deviance and crime.
12.	D	152	The wrongdoing of wealthy and powerful individuals and organizations is known as both elite deviance and corporate deviance.
13.	B	153	Macrosociological theories of deviance include conflict theory.
14.	C	153	Differential association theory interprets deviance, including criminal behavior, as behavior one learns through interaction with others.
15.	A	154	The definition a person has of himself or herself as a deviant is their deviant identity.
16.	D	152	Elite deviance includes illegal arrangements made for corporate profit, illegal campaign contributions, and government actions that abuse public trust, such as secret arms deals or lying about covert activity.
17.	C	154	A deviant career is the sequence of movements a person makes through different positions in an occupational system.
18.	A	155	Groups that are organized around particular forms of social deviance are deviant communities.
19.	D	155	Labeling theorists argue that official statistics reflect social judgments, not necessarily the actual commission of crimes or deviant acts. Labeling theorists are more likely to ask how behavior becomes labeled deviant than they are to ask what motivates people to become deviant. Labeling theorists believe that official rape rates are underestimates of the actual extent of rape.
20.	A	156	Those people with the fewest resources are most likely to be labeled mentally ill.
21.	B	157	A stigma is an attribute that is socially devalued and discredited.
22.	C	158	Larceny is included in the *Uniform Crime Report*.
23.	A	158	Illicit activities, such as gambling, illegal drug use and prostitution, in which there is no complainant, are victimless crimes.
24.	D	159	Crime which is committed by organized groups and typically involves the provision of illegal goods and services to others is organized crime.
25.	C	158	White-collar crime seldom generates great concern in the public mind.
26.	D	161	Police discretion is greatest when dealing with minor offenses, such as disorderly

44

conduct. Police discretion is strongly influenced by class and race judgments. Minority communities are policed much more intensively than White communities, which leads to more frequent arrests for those who live in minority communities.

27.	B	151	Conflict theories of deviance, based on the work of Karl Marx, use the macrosociological approach, since they examine the structure of society as a whole in their explanation of deviance.
28.	A	152	Social control agents are those who regulate and administer the societal response to deviance, such as the police and mental health workers.
29.	C	158	*The Uniform Crime Report* is published annually in the United States by the Federal Bureau of Investigation.
30.	D	158	Hate crimes are assaults and other malicious acts directed against gay men, lesbian women, people with disabilities, and racial minorities.

ANSWERS TO THE TRUE-FALSE STATEMENTS.

1.	T	144	Durkheim argued that societies need deviance in order to understand what normal behavior is.
2.	T	147	Sociologists criticize the medicalization of deviance for ignoring the effects of social structures on the development of deviant behavior.
3.	F	147	Durkheim's investigation of suicide identified the critical importance of social factors rather than psychological factors as causes of deviant behavior.
4.	T	149	Sociologists have linked the condition of anomie to a variety of social problems, including juvenile delinquency.
5.	F	149	According to the structural strain theory, a prostitute has accepted the cultural values of the dominant society, since s/he wishes to be economically successful and accepts the commercialization of sexuality that characterizes the dominant culture.
6.	T	152	Conflict theorists argue that members of the upper class can better hide crimes because they have the resources to mask their deviance and crimes.
7.	T	157	A disability may become the master status for a disabled person. Through this process, the disability overrides all other features of the person's identity.
8.	F	157	Crime is one form of deviance.
9.	F	158	Enforcement of victimless crimes is typically not as vigorous as the enforcement of crimes against persons or property, although periodic crackdowns occur, such as the current trend toward mandatory sentencing for drug violations.
10.	T	159	Certain groups are more likely to commit crime than others, because crime is distinctively linked to patterns of inequality in society.
11.	T	161	Racial minority groups are far more likely than Whites to be poor, unemployed, and living in single-parent families and these social factors are predictors of a higher rate of crime.
12.	T	161	Women's participation in crime has been increasing in recent years.
13.	F	162	Women are less likely to be victimized by crime than men, although victimization by crime among women varies significantly by race and age.
14.	T	162	Women's fear of crime increases with age, although the likelihood of victimization decreases with age.
15.	T	166	In general, prisons seem neither to deter crime nor rehabilitate criminals.

Chapter Seven

SOCIAL STRATIFICATION

Multiple-Choice Statements. Select the best response.

1. Which of the following statements about inequality in the United States is (are) TRUE?
    a.   In 1977, nearly one-fifth of American children lived in poverty, including 37% of Hispanic and African American children.
    b.   Black family income is 62% of White family income.
    c.   One percent of the U.S. population controls 39 percent of total household wealth.
    d.   All of the above

2. _____ is the process by which different statuses in any group, organization, or society develop.
    a.   Social differentiation
    b.   Social stratification
    c.   Social hierarchy development
    d.   Social estate creation

3. A(n) _____ system of stratification is one in which the ownership of property and the exercise of power is monopolized by an elite who have total control over societal resources.
    a.   caste
    b.   class
    c.   estate
    d.   status

4. The system of apartheid in South Africa, in which the travel, employment, associations, and place of residence of Black Africans were severely restricted, is an example of a(n):
    a.   caste
    b.   class
    c.   estate
    d.   status

5. The social structural position groups hold relative to the economic, social, political, and cultural resources of a society is:
    a.   social status
    b.   social class
    c.   social stratification
    d.   social power

6. Max Weber described the consequences of stratification as _____, meaning the opportunities that people have in common by virtue of belonging to a particular class.
    a.   life opportunities
    b.   class benefits
    c.   differential advantages
    d.   life chances

7. Which of the following is (are) used by sociologists as indicators of social class?
    a.   education
    b.   occupation
    c.   income
    d.   all of the above

46

8. In Marx's analysis, two primary classes exist under capitalism. Those who own the means of production comprise the:
    a. working class
    b. proletariat
    c. lumpenproletariat
    d. bourgeoisie

9. _____ refers to belief systems that support the status quo.
    a. False consciousness
    b. Class consciousness
    c. Ideology
    d. Social differentiation

10. Weber defined _____ as the economic dimension of stratification, which determines how much access to material goods that a group or individual has. This is measured by income, property, and other financial assets.
    a. class
    b. status
    c. party
    d. wealth

11. According to Weber, the capacity to influence groups and individuals even in the face of opposition is:
    a. class
    b. status
    c. party
    d. power

12. Which of the following statements about the functionalist perspective is (are) TRUE?
    a. Inequality results from a system of domination and subordination where those with the most resources exploit and control others.
    b. The most vital jobs in society (those that sustain life and the quality of life) are usually the least rewarded.
    c. Those who work hardest and succeed have greater life chances.
    d. All of the above

13. _____ is a person's movement over time from one class to another.
    a. Social mobility
    b. Social change
    c. Social promotion
    d. Social advancement

14. The process by which people end up in a given position in the stratification system is:
    a. status achievement
    b. status attainment
    c. discrimination
    d. conflict

15. Income, occupational prestige, and education are the three measures of _____ that have been found to be the most significant in determining people's placement in the U.S. stratification system.
    a. social class
    b. social status
    c. social differentiation
    d. socioeconomic status (SES)

16. The value assigned to people and groups by others is:
   a. prestige
   b. social class
   c. status
   d. social stratification

17. The amount of money that is brought into a household from various sources, including wages, investment incomes, and dividends, during a given period is:
   a. wealth
   b. salary
   c. income
   d. never enough

18. Which of the following is (are) among the occupations considered to have the lowest prestige in the U.S.?
   a. newspaper columnist
   b. janitor
   c. insurance agent
   d. all of the above

19. Those in the upper class with newly acquired wealth are known as the:
   a. upwardly mobile
   b. YUPPIES
   c. nouveau riche
   d. new management team

20. The _____ includes those who have been left behind by contemporary economic development and who are likely to be unemployed and therefore dependent on public assistance or crime for economic support.
   a. underclass
   b. lower class
   c. dregs of society
   d. downwardly mobile

21. Marx defined the working class as those who sell their labor for:
   a. benefits
   b. financial security
   c. salaries
   d. wages

22. _____ is calculated by adding all financial assets, such as stocks, bonds, property, and insurance, and subtracting debts.
   a. Wealth
   b. Median income
   c. Net worth
   d. a and c

23. When children achieve a significantly different class status than parents, which of the following has occurred?
   a. intergenerational mobility
   b. crossgenerational mobility
   c. intragenerational mobility
   d. familial mobility

48

24.	_____ is both the perception that a class structure exists and the feeling of shared identification with others in one's class, or others with whom one perceives common life chances.
	a.	False consciousness
	b.	Class identification
	c.	Class consciousness
	d.	Class awareness

25.	In the United States, the _____ is the amount of money needed to support the basic needs of the household, as determined by the federal government.
	a.	subsistence level
	b.	poverty line
	c.	survival level
	d.	minimum wage

26.	The term _____ refers to the increasing proportion of the poor who are women and children.
	a.	the new face of poverty
	b.	gendered nature of poverty
	c.	the changing poverty demographic
	d.	feminization of poverty

27.	Which of the following statements about poverty in the U.S. is (are) TRUE?
	a.	The vast majority of the poor have always been women and children, but their proportion of the poor has been increasing in recent years.
	b.	One of the marked changes in poverty is the location of poverty in metropolitan areas, particularly central cities.
	c.	Some of the poor are homeless, who were released from mental hospitals as a result of the deinstitutionalization movement of the 1970s.
	d.	All of the above

28.	According to the _____ argument, the major causes of poverty are welfare dependency, the absence of work values, and the irresponsibility of the poor.
	a.	structural-strain
	b.	culture of poverty
	c.	conflict
	d.	symbolic interactionist

29.	In the hierarchy of social classes, the _____ class includes workers in the skilled trades and low-income bureaucratic workers, such as secretaries, police personnel, and firefighters.
	a.	nouveau riche
	b.	lower
	c.	lower middle
	d.	middle

30.	Karl Marx used the term _____ to describe the class consciousness of subordinate classes who had internalized the view of the dominant class.
	a.	ideology
	b.	dominant ideology
	c.	false consciousness
	d.	identification with the bourgeoisie

True-False Statements.

1. To sociologists, life chances are the result of social structural arrangements. Class membership determines how well one is served by such social institutions as education, health care, etc.

2. In a caste system of stratification, one's place is an achieved status.

3. Marx argued that with the development of capitalism, the capitalists and the working class would become increasingly antagonistic and polarized.

4. According to the conflict perspective, social inequality serves to motivate people to fill the different positions in society that are needed for the survival of society.

5. The best predictor of an individual's future wealth in the U.S. is the amount of education the person has achieved.

6. By far the majority of Americans identify themselves as upper class, even though they vary widely in lifestyle and in resources at their disposal.

7. In recent years, both the African American and Latino middle class have expanded, primarily as the result of increased access to education and middle-class occupations for people of color.

8. Sociological research has found that intergenerational upward mobility characterizes the majority of families in the U.S.

9. Those who are upwardly mobile are often expected to distance themselves from their origins.

10. Compared to most other nations in the world, the U.S. is affluent.

11. Nearly 15 percent of all poor families in the U.S. are headed by women.

12. Most of the able-bodied poor are employed.

13. The Personal Responsibility and Work Reconciliation Act stipulates a lifetime limit of twelve years for people to receive welfare and requires all welfare recipients, through a policy known as workfare, to find work within four years.

14. Caste systems of stratification are most common in agricultural societies.

15. Eighteen percent of the U.S. population has no health insurance.

Short-Answer Questions.
A page reference to the relevant text material is provided in the parenthesis.

1. Define social stratification. Describe and provide one example of each of the following stratification systems: estate, caste, and class (172).

2. List and discuss the three dimensions of stratification, according to Weber (175).

3. List and discuss each of the five social classes which exist in the United States, according to the textbook (179).

4. Define social mobility and discuss its extent in the U.S. (186).

5. Compare and contrast the culture of poverty explanation of poverty with the theory of structural causes

50

(191).

ANSWERS TO THE MULTIPLE-CHOICE QUESTIONS.

1.	D	171	In 1977, nearly one-fifth of American children lived in poverty, including 37% of Hispanic and African American children. Black family income is 62% of White family income. One percent of the U.S. population controls 39 percent of total household wealth.
2.	A	172	Social differentiation is the process by which different statuses in any group, organization, or society develop.
3.	C	172	An estate system of stratification is one in which the ownership of property and the exercise of power is monopolized by an elite who have total control over societal resources.
4.	A	173	The system of apartheid in South Africa, in which the travel, employment, associations, and place of residence of Black Africans were severely restricted, is an example of a caste.
5.	B	153	The social structural position groups hold relative to the economic, social, political, and cultural resources of a society is social class.
6.	D	173	Max Weber described the consequences of stratification as life chances, meaning the opportunities that people have in common by virtue of belonging to a particular class.
7.	D	173	Education, occupation, and income are used by sociologists as indicators of social class.
8.	B	174	In Marx's analysis, two primary classes exist under capitalism. Those who own the means of production comprise the proletariat.
9.	C	174	Ideology refers to belief systems that support the status quo.
10.	A	175	Weber defined class as the economic dimension of stratification, which determines how much access to material goods that a group or individual has. This is measured by income, property, and other financial assets.
11.	C	175	According to Weber, the capacity to influence groups and individuals even in the face of opposition is party.
12.	C	176	According to functionalist theorists, those who work hardest and succeed have greater life chances.
13.	A	177	Social mobility is a person's movement over time from one class to another.
14.	B	178	The process by which people end up in a given position in the stratification system is status attainment.
15.	D	178	Income, occupational prestige, and education are the three measures of socioeconomic status (SES) that have been found to be the most significant in determining people's placement in the U.S. stratification system.
16.	A	178	The value assigned to people and groups by others is prestige.
17.	C	182	The amount of money that is brought into a household from various sources, including wages, investment incomes, and dividends, during a given period is income.
18.	B	178	Janitors are among the occupations considered to have the lowest prestige in the U.S.
19.	C	179	Those in the upper class with newly acquired wealth are known as the nouveau riche.
20.	A	180	The underclass includes those who have been left behind by contemporary economic development and who are likely to be unemployed and therefore dependent on public assistance or crime for economic support.
21.	D	181	Marx defined the working class as those who sell their labor for wages.
22.	D	182	Wealth and net worth are calculated by adding all financial assets, such as stocks, bonds, property, and insurance, and subtracting debts.
23.	A	186	When children achieve a significantly different class status than parents, intergenerational mobility has occurred.
24.	C	187	Class consciousness is both the perception that a class structure exists and the feeling of shared identification with others in one's class, or others with whom one perceives common life chances.
25.	B	188	In the United States, the poverty line is the amount of money needed to support the basic needs of the household, as determined by the federal government.

26.	D	188	The term feminization of poverty refers to the increasing proportion of the poor who are women and children.
27.	D	188	The vast majority of the poor have always been women and children, but their proportion of the poor has been increasing in recent years. One of the marked changes in poverty is the location of poverty in metropolitan areas, particularly central cities. Some of the poor are homeless, who were released from mental hospitals as a result of the deinstitutionalization movement of the 1970s.
28.	B	189	According to the culture of poverty argument, the major causes of poverty are welfare dependency, the absence of work values, and the irresponsibility of the poor.
29.	C	180	In the hierarchy of social classes, the lower middle class includes workers in the skilled trades and low-income bureaucratic workers, such as secretaries, police personnel, and firefighters.
30.	C	187	Karl Marx used the term false consciousness to describe the class consciousness of subordinate classes who had internalized the view of the dominant class.

ANSWERS TO THE TRUE-FALSE STATEMENTS.

1.	T	173	To sociologists, life chances are the result of social structural arrangements. Class membership determines how well one is served by such social institutions as education, health care, etc.
2.	F	173	In a caste system of stratification, one's place is an ascribed status.
3.	T	174	Marx argued that with the development of capitalism, the capitalists and the working class would become increasingly antagonistic and polarized.
4.	F	176	According to the functionalist perspective, social inequality serves to motivate people to fill the different positions in society that are needed for the survival of society.
5.	F	179	The best predictor of an individual's future wealth in the U.S. is the class status of the family into which they were born.
6.	F	179	By far the majority of Americans identify themselves as middle class, even though they vary widely in lifestyle and in resources at their disposal.
7.	T	184	In recent years, both the African American and Latino middle class have expanded, primarily as the result of increased access to education and middle-class occupations for people of color.
8.	F	186	Sociological research has found that intergenerational upward mobility is much more limited than the American dream suggests.
9.	T	186	Those who are upwardly mobile are often expected to distance themselves from their origins.
10.	T	187	Compared to most other nations in the world, the U.S. is affluent.
11.	F	188	More than half of all poor families in the U.S. are headed by women.
12.	T	191	Most of the able-bodied poor are employed.
13.	F	193	The Personal Responsibility and Work Reconciliation Act stipulates a lifetime limit of five years for people to receive welfare and requires all welfare recipients, through a policy known as workfare, to find work within two years.
14.	F	172	Estate systems of stratification are most common in agricultural societies.
15.	T	171	Eighteen percent of the U.S. population has no health insurance.

Chapter Eight

GLOBAL STRATIFICATION

Multiple-Choice Questions. Select the best response.

1. According to sociologists, each nation is part of a(n) _____ in which its position substantially is determined by its relationship to other countries in the world.
    a. international system of economic interdependence
    b. global stratification system
    c. global village
    d. global system of internationalism

2. The per capita GNP (gross national product):
    a. is reliable only in countries that are based on a cash economy
    b. measures informal exchanges or bartering in which resources are exchanged without money changing hands
    c. is reliable only in countries that are not based on a cash economy
    d. b and c

3. Those countries which are largely rural, poor, underdeveloped, and have high levels of poverty are:
    a. core countries
    b. first-world countries
    c. third-world countries
    d. second-world countries

4. According to Anthony Marx, different countries develop different definitions of _____, which strongly affect how members are treated.
    a. race
    b. gender
    c. social class
    d. none of the above

5. The ability of a country to exercise control over other countries or groups of countries is:
    a. government
    b. negotiation
    c. directly related to population size and density
    d. power

6. Cheap labor:
    a. is usually found in non-Western countries
    b. is an important component of the new international division of labor
    c. has created a poor and dependent workforce that is mostly people of color
    d. all of the above

7. Over half of the world's population:
    a. live in the wealthiest countries
    b. live in the poorest countries
    c. live in countries with the highest death rates
    d. b and c

8. Modernization theory:
   a. focuses on the processes and results of European colonization and imperialism
   b. views the economic development of a country as a worldwide process involving nearly all countries that have been affected by technological change
   c. focuses on explaining the persistence of poverty in the world
   d. a and c

9. Dependency theory:
   a. suggests that multinational corporations play a role in keeping dependent nations poor
   b. has been criticized because it posits that governments should not be involved in making economic decisions or policies that restrict free trade or business activities
   c. is closely associated with the work of Immanuel Wallerstein
   d. all of the above

10. According to worlds systems theory, the rich, powerful, industrialized countries that control the system are the:
    a. semi-peripheral countries
    b. peripheral countries
    c. core countries
    d. third-world countries

11. Which of the following countries, based on per capita GNP, is (are) among the richest in the world?
    a. Singapore
    b. Japan
    c. Iceland
    d. All of the above

12. Which of the following countries, based on per capita GNP, is (are) are among the ten poorest in the world?
    a. Iceland
    b. Ethiopia
    c. Luxembourg
    d. All of the above

13. The system of classifying nations, which was based on the politics of the cold war, divided countries into:
    a. core, semi-peripheral, and peripheral countries
    b. first-world, second-world, and third-world countries
    c. democratic, socialist, and communist countries
    d. industrialized, agricultural, and horticultural countries

14. Using power as a dimension, the countries of the world can be divided into three levels based on their position in the world economic system. These levels include:
    a. core, semi-peripheral, and peripheral countries
    b. first-world, second-world, and third-world countries
    c. democratic, socialist, and communist countries
    d. industrialized, agricultural, and horticultural countries

15. Variables which are considered indicators of basic living conditions in countries throughout the world include:
    a. percentage of females who are literate
    b. crude birthrate
    c. life expectancy at birth (in years)
    d. all of the above

16. According to world systems theorists, the network of production and labor processes by which a product becomes a finished commodity is called the:
    a. commodity chain
    b. international manufacturing process
    c. multinational assembly line
    d. segmented system of production

17. Using the standard of _____, households in poverty in the United States are poor compared with other Americans, but when one looks at other parts of the world, an income of $16,4000. would make a family very well off.
    a. capability poverty
    b. absolute poverty
    c. relative poverty
    d. psychological poverty

18. _____ is defined as the situation in which people live on less than $275. a year (or less than 75 cents a day).
    a. world poverty
    b. extreme poverty
    c. capability poverty
    d. relative poverty

19. Using the United Nations' definition of world poverty, almost half of the people living in poverty live in:
    a. South Asia
    b. Central Africa
    c. Central America
    d. North Africa

20. As with poverty in the United States, women bear a larger share of the burden of world poverty. Some theorists refer to this as:
    a. gender-based poverty
    b. dependent poverty
    c. gender discrimination
    d. double deprivation

21. Which of the following statements is (are) TRUE?
    a. Fertility rates are higher in poor countries.
    b. Most, though not all, poor countries are matriarchal, meaning that women control the household.
    c. The United Nations Commission on the Status of Women estimates that women constitute nearly 40 percent of the world's population.
    d. All of the above.

22. According to *The State of World Hunger*, _____ occurs when households cannot afford to purchase enough food to adequately feed the members of the household.
    a. food shortage
    b. food poverty
    c. food deprivation
    d. starvation

23. According to *The State of World Hunger*, _____ refers to the inadequate food consumption of individuals to maintain a healthy life.
    a. food shortage
    b. food poverty
    c. food deprivation
    d. malnutrition

24.   The newly industrializing countries (NICs) include:
        a.   Korea
        b.   Thailand
        c.   Singapore
        d.   All of the above

25.   _____ is a system of inequality of the distribution of resources and opportunities between countries.
        a.   International inequity
        b.   Global inequality
        c.   Global stratification
        d.   Capitalism

26.   According to the World Bank, which country had the highest per capita GNP in 1998 U.S. dollars?
        a.   Germany
        b.   Luxembourg
        c.   The United States
        d.   Iceland

27.   According to the World Bank, which country had the lowest per capita GNP in 1998 U.S. dollars?
        a.   Niger
        b.   Republic of Congo
        c.   Chad
        d.   Ethiopia

28.   The industrialized capitalist countries of the world are:
        a.   first-world countries
        b.   second-world countries
        c.   third-world countries
        d.   peripheral countries

29.   Countries with a communist-based government and a state-managed economy, with free education, health care, and low-cost housing, are:

        a.   first-world countries
        b.   second-world countries
        c.   third-world countries
        d.   peripheral countries

30.   Those countries that extract profits from the poor countries and pass the profit on to core countries are:
        a.   semi-peripheral countries
        b.   peripheral countries
        c.   first-world countries
        d.   third-world countries

31.   Spain, Turkey, and Mexico are considered:
        a.   peripheral countries
        b.   first-world countries
        c.   semi-peripheral countries
        d.   third-world countries

32. More than 62 percent of the people in the world live in countries:
    a.   where the death rate is low and the birth rate is high
    b.   where the death rate is high and the birth rate is low
    c.   where the average income is less than $1000. per year
    d.   with a high primary school enrollment ratio

33. The richest countries of the world have approximately _____- percent of the world's population.
    a.   14
    b.   31
    c.   52
    d.   67

34. The theory of global stratification which is an outgrowth of functionalism and Weber's concept of the Protestant Ethic is:
    a.   dependency theory
    b.   world systems theory
    c.   the neocolonialism theory
    d.   modernization theory

35. The theory of global stratification derived from the work of Karl Marx is:
    a.   dependency theory
    b.   world systems theory
    c.   the neocolonialism theory
    d.   modernization theory

36. _____ argues that no nation can be seen in isolation. There is a world economic system that must be understood as a single unit.
    a.   Dependency theory
    b.   World systems theory
    c.   The neocolonialism theory
    d.   Modernization theory

37. Poor countries, which are largely agricultural and are manipulated by the core countries, which extract resources and profits from them, are:
    a.   semi-peripheral countries
    b.   peripheral countries
    c.   first-world countries
    d.   second-world countries

38. _____ is a form of control of poor countries by rich countries, without direct political or military involvement.
    a.   Dependency
    b.   Capitalism
    c.   Neocolonialism
    d.   Socialism

39. Among the essential human requirements to survive is (are):
    a.   nourishment
    b.   the ability to reproduce
    c.   education
    d.   all of the above

40. _____ is the situation in which human beings do not have enough money for basic survival.
   a. Relative poverty
   b. Capability poverty
   c. Absolute poverty
   d. Malnutrition

True-False Statements.

1. In the high-income nations of the world, education is almost universal.

2. According to *The State of World Hunger*, food shortage, food poverty, and food deprivation are interrelated.

3. Hunger has substantially increased worldwide. While 20 percent of the people of the world were chronically underfed in 1970, by 1990 36 percent were chronically underfed.

4. Poverty can be caused by incompetent or bankrupted governments as well as by changes in the world economic system.

5. The oil-rich countries of the Middle East are considered second-world countries.

6. The rich core countries that dominate the world system are largely European, with the addition of the United States and Japan. The populations of these countries, with the exception of Japan, are mostly White.

7. The vast majority of people who suffer from malnutrition and hunger worldwide are people of color.

8. In the poorest nations, only 88 percent of women are literate, women live 8 percent longer than men, and very few women die in childbirth.

9. Dependency theory, first proposed during the 1960s, was developed to explain why some countries had achieved economic development and why some had not.

10. Modernization theory ignores that the development of a country may be due to its economic relationships with other more powerful countries.

11. Each day, an estimated 30,000 people die as a consequence of chronic, persistent hunger.

12. Tragically, the world's production of wheat, rice, corn, and other grains is insufficient to feed all of the people in the world.

13. Dependency theory argues that for economic development to occur, countries must change their traditional attitudes, values, and institutions.

14. Multinational corporations recognize no national boundaries and pursue business where they can best make a profit.

15. According to world systems theory, the countries in Latin America are mostly semi-peripheral countries.

Short-Answer Questions.

A page reference to the relevant text material is provided in the parenthesis.

1. List three indicators of basic living conditions, related to health, which are used to compare nations with different per capita GNPs (205).

2.	Define and briefly describe the following terms: first-world, second-world, and third-world countries. List three examples of each (202).

3.	List and discuss the three theories of global stratification which are discussed in the textbook (207).

4.	Define and describe the following terms: relative poverty, absolute poverty, world poverty, extreme poverty, and capability poverty (212).

5.	List and describe the three-part typology of countries, based on their position in the world economic system, which uses power as the dimension of stratification (203).

6.	What are the effects of a high fertility rate on the quality of life in a country (205)?

7.	Describe the differences in health between high-income countries and low-income countries (206).

8.	Describe the differences in education between high-income countries and low-income countries (206).

9.	Discuss the multinational process of manufacturing toys. How does this affect the cost and selection of toys in the United States (211)?

10.	Which theory of global stratification is similar to the culture of poverty theory? Discuss the similarity (208).

ANSWERS TO MULTIPLE-CHOICE QUESTIONS.

1.	B	199	According to sociologists, each nation is part of a global stratification system in which its position substantially is determined by its relationship to other countries in the world.
2.	A	200	The per capita GNP (gross national product) is reliable only in countries that are based on a cash economy.
3.	C	202	Those countries which are largely rural, poor, underdeveloped, and have high levels of poverty are third-world countries.
4.	A	204	According to Anthony Marx, different countries develop different definitions of race, which strongly affect how members are treated.
5.	D	205	The ability of a country to exercise control over other countries or groups of countries is power.
6.	D	206	Cheap labor is usually found in non-Western countries, is an important component of the new international division of labor, and has created a poor and dependent workforce that is mostly people of color.
7.	D	204	Over half of the world's population live in the poorest countries, with the highest death rates.
8.	B	207	Modernization theory views the economic development of a country as a worldwide process involving nearly all countries that have been affected by technological change.
9.	A	210	Dependency theory suggests that multinational corporations play a role in keeping dependent nations poor.
10.	C	211	According to worlds systems theory, the rich, powerful, industrialized countries that control the system are the core countries.
11.	D	201	Singapore, Japan, and Iceland, based on per capita GNP, are among the richest in the world.
12.	B	202	Ethiopia, based on per capita GNP, is are among the ten poorest in the world.
13.	B	202	The system of classifying nations, which was based on the politics of the cold war, divided countries into first-world, second-world, and third-world countries.
14.	A	203	Using power as a dimension, the countries of the world can be divided into three levels based on their position in the world economic system. These levels include core, semi-peripheral, and peripheral countries.

15.	D	205	Variables which are considered indicators of basic living conditions in countries throughout the world include percentage of females who are literate, crude birthrate, and life expectancy at birth (in years).
16.	A	211	According to world systems theorists, the network of production and labor processes by which a product becomes a finished commodity is called the commodity chain.
17.	C	212	Using the standard of relative poverty, households in poverty in the United States are poor compared with other Americans, but when one looks at other parts of the world, an income of $16,4000. would make a family very well off.
18.	B	212	Extreme poverty is defined as the situation in which people live on less than $275. a year (or less than 75 cents a day).
19.	A	212	Using the United Nations' definition of world poverty, almost half of the people living in poverty live in South Asia.
20.	D	213	As with poverty in the United States, women bear a larger share of the burden of world poverty. Some theorists refer to this as double deprivation.
21.	A	213	Fertility rates are higher in poor countries.
22.	A	214	According to *The State of World Hunger*, food shortage occurs when households cannot afford to purchase enough food to adequately feed the members of the household.
23.	C	214	According to *The State of World Hunger*, food deprivation refers to the inadequate food consumption of individuals to maintain a healthy life.
24.	D	216	The newly industrializing countries (NICs) include Korea, Thailand, and Singapore.
25.	C	199	Global stratification is a system of inequality of the distribution of resources and opportunities between countries.
26.	B	201	According to the World Bank, Luxembourg had the highest per capita GNP in 1998 U.S. dollars.
27.	B	202	According to the World Bank, the Republic of Congo had the lowest per capita GNP in 1998 U.S. dollars.
28.	A	202	The industrialized capitalist countries of the world are first-world countries.
29.	B	202	Countries with a communist-based government and a state-managed economy, with free education, health care, and low-cost housing, are second-world countries.
30.	A	203	Those countries that extract profits from the poor countries and pass the profit on to core countries are semi-peripheral countries.
31.	C	203	Spain, Turkey, and Mexico are considered semi-peripheral countries.
32.	C	205	More than 62 percent of the people in the world live in countries where the average income is less than $1000. per year.
33.	A	205	The richest countries of the world have approximately 14 percent of the world's population.
34.	D	207	The theory of global stratification which is an outgrowth of functionalism and Weber's concept of the Protestant Ethic is modernization theory.
35.	A	209	The theory of global stratification derived from the work of Karl Marx is dependency theory.
36.	B	210	World systems theory argues that no nation can be seen in isolation. There is a world economic system that must be understood as a single unit.
37.	B	211	Poor countries, which are largely agricultural and are manipulated by the core countries, which extract resources and profits from them, are peripheral countries.
38.	C	210	Neocolonialism is a form of control of poor countries by rich countries, without direct political or military involvement.
39.	D	217	Among the essential human requirements to survive are nourishment, the ability to reproduce, and education.
40.	C	212	Absolute poverty is the situation in which human beings do not have enough money for basic survival.

ANSWERS TO TRUE-FALSE STATEMENTS.

| 1. | T | 206 | In the high-income nations of the world, education is almost universal. |

2.	T	214	According to *The State of World Hunger*, food shortage, food poverty, and food deprivation are interrelated.
3.	F	215	Most areas of the world showed a marked decrease in hunger. While 36 percent of the people of the world were chronically underfed in 1970, by 1990 only 20 percent were chronically underfed.
4.	T	215	Poverty can be caused by incompetent or bankrupted governments as well as by changes in the world economic system.
5.	F	202	The oil-rich countries of the Middle East are not part of the first-world or second-world, but they also do not belong in the same category as the poor countries of Asia and Africa.
6.	T	203	The rich core countries that dominate the world system are largely European, with the addition of the United States and Japan. The populations of these countries, with the exception of Japan, are mostly White.
7.	T	204	The vast majority of people who suffer from malnutrition and hunger worldwide are people of color.
8.	F	207	In the richest nations, 88 percent of women are literate, women live 8 percent longer than men, and very few women die in childbirth.
9.	F	207	Modernization theory, first proposed during the 1960s, was developed to explain why some countries had achieved economic development and why some had not.
10.	T	217	Modernization theory ignores that the development of a country may be due to its economic relationships with other more powerful countries.
11.	T	213	Each day, an estimated 30,000 people die as a consequence of chronic, persistent hunger.
12.	F	214	The world's production of wheat, rice, corn, and other grains is sufficient to feed all of the people in the world. The problem is that surplus food in the world does not get to the truly needy.
13.	F	207	Modernization theory argues that for economic development to occur, countries must change their traditional attitudes, values, and institutions.
14.	T	210	Multinational corporations recognize no national boundaries and pursue business where they can best make a profit.
15.	F	211	According to world systems theory, the countries in Latin America are mostly peripheral countries.

Chapter Nine

RACE AND ETHNICITY

MULTIPLE-Choice Questions. Select the best response.

1. A(n) _____ is a social category of people who share a common culture, a common language or dialect, religion, norms, customs, and history.
   a. minority group
   b. ethnic group
   c. dominant group
   d. race

2. A _____ is a group treated as distinct in society on the basis of certain characteristics, some of which are biological, that have been assigned social importance in society.
   a. ethnic group
   b. minority group
   c. race
   d. dominant group

3. _____ is the process by which a group comes to be defined as a race.
   a. Racial formation
   b. Racial construction
   c. Racism
   d. Assimilation

4. The group that assigns a racial or ethnic group to subordinate status in society is called the:
   a. dominant group
   b. peer group
   c. social majority
   d. a and c

5. In general, a racial or ethnic minority group has which of the following characteristics?
   a. It suffers prejudice and discrimination by the dominant group.
   b. Membership in the group is frequently ascribed rather than achieved.
   c. Members of a minority group feel a strong sense of solidarity.
   d. All of the above

6. Italian Americans, Japanese Americans, Arab Americans, Serbians and Croatians in Bosnia, and the tribal Hutus and Tutsis in Rwanda are examples of:
   a. dominant groups
   b. countercultures
   c. races
   d. ethnic groups

7. Which of the following statements about race is (are) TRUE?
   a. The categories used to divide groups into races are fixed, on the basis of skin color and hair texture.
   b. Different groups use virtually identical criteria to define racial groups.
   c. The biological differences that are presumed to define different racial groups are somewhat arbitrary.
   d. a and b

8.   A(n) _____ is an oversimplified set of beliefs about members of a social group or social stratum that is used to categorize individuals of that group.
       a.   scapegoat
       b.   stereotype
       c.   ideology
       d.   false consciousness

9.   The evaluation of a social group, and individuals within that group, based on conceptions about the social group that are held despite facts that contradict it and that involve both prejudgment and misjudgment is:
       a.   prejudice
       b.   discrimination
       c.   ethnocentrism
       d.   racism

10.   _____ is the belief that one's group is superior to all other groups.
       a.   Racism
       b.   Ethnocentrism
       c.   Prejudice
       d.   Discrimination

11.   The overt negative and unequal treatment of the members of some social group or stratum solely because of their membership in that group or stratum is:
       a.   discrimination
       b.   racism
       c.   ethnocentrism
       d.   prejudice

12.   A(n) _____ is any distinct group in society that shares common group characteristics and is forced to occupy low status in society because of prejudice and discrimination.
       a.   ethnic group
       b.   racial group
       c.   minority group
       d.   reference group

13.   The categorization of people into groups and the subsequent applications of stereotypes are based on the _____, which states that we categorize people on the basis of what appears initially prominent and obvious about them.
       a.   salience principle
       b.   repeated behavior principle
       c.   past experiences with group members
       d.   all of the above

14.   The principle of _____ holds that stereotypes, especially negative ones, are often able to be applied to different social classes, racial and ethnic groups, and gender groups.
       a.   salience
       b.   scapegoating
       c.   stereotype interchangeability
       d.   ethnocentrism

15.   The spatial separation of racial and ethnic groups into different neighborhoods is:
       a.   community segregation
       b.   residential segregation
       c.   household segregation
       d.   not evident in most U.S. communities

16. The negative treatment and oppression of one racial or ethnic group by society's existing institutions based on the presumed inferiority of the oppressed group is:
    a. ethnocentrism
    b. cultural pluralism
    c. institutional discrimination
    d. institutional racism

17. _____ theory argues that, historically, members of the dominant group in the U.S. have harbored various frustrations in their desire to achieve social and economic success.
    a. Scapegoat
    b. Functionalist
    c. Conflict
    d. Symbolic interaction

18. According to Adorno et. al., the _____ is characterized by a tendency to rigidly characterize other people, as well as tendencies to submit to authority, rigidly conform, be very intolerant of ambiguity, and be inclined to superstition.
    a. discriminator
    b. racist
    c. authoritarian personality
    d. prejudiced person

19. The process by which a minority becomes, socially, economically, and culturally absorbed within the dominant society is:
    a. integration
    b. assimilation
    c. absorption
    d. miscegenation

20. Which of the following statements about the interaction between Whites and minorities which will reduce prejudice is (are) TRUE, according to contact theorists?
    a. The contact must be between individuals of equal status.
    b. The contact between equals must be sustained.
    c. Social norms favoring equality must be agreed upon by the participants.
    d. All of the above.

21. The _____ theory investigates the interaction or combined effects of race and sex in the oppression of women of color.
    a. racist sexism
    b. double jeopardy
    c. gendered racism
    d. feminist

22. The minority group which has the highest poverty rate in the United States is:
    a. African Americans
    b. Native Americans
    c. Mexican Americans
    d. Asian Americans

23. Persons with the _____ perspective believe that to overcome adversity and oppression, the minority person needs to imitate the dominant White culture as much as possible.
    a. assimilationist
    b. cultural pluralism
    c. acculturalist
    d. blending

24. Different groups in a society which maintain their distinctive cultures while coexisting with the dominant group characterize:
    a.   assimilation
    b.   acculturation
    c.   integration
    d.   cultural pluralism

25. The spatial and social segregation of racial and ethnic groups is:
    a.   racism
    b.   integration
    c.   segregation
    d.   discrimination

26. The refusal of _____ to relinquish her seat in the "White only" section on a segregated bus began the Montgomery Bus Boycott in 1955.
    a.   Rosa Parks
    b.   Coretta Scott king
    c.   Harriett Tubman
    d.   Barbara Jordan

27. _____ policies are those that recognize the unique status of racial groups because of the long history of discrimination and the continuing influence of institutional racism.
    a.   Anti-discrimination
    b.   Race-specific
    c.   Racial equity
    d.   Affirmative action

28. A controversial program for change to reduce job and educational inequality is known as:
    a.   affirmative action
    b.   change for equity
    c.   equality for all Americans
    d.   racial and gender equality

29. Which of the following statements about the Black power movement is (are) TRUE?
    a.   The Black power movement of the 1960s rejected assimilation and demanded self-determination and self-regulation of Black communities.
    b.   Many of the leaders of the Black power movement were eliminated, through assassinations, imprisonment, or other means.
    c.   The Black power movement argued that racial inequality was rooted in the institutional power that Whites and over Black Americans.
    d.   All of the above

30. Which of the following statements about ethnic groups is (are) TRUE?
    a.   Ethnic groups can develop more or less intense ethnic identification at different points in time.
    b.   Ethnic identification may grow stronger when groups face prejudice or hostility from other groups.
    c.   Ethnic unity can develop voluntarily or may be imposed when ethnic groups are excluded by more powerful groups from certain residential areas, occupations, or social clubs.
    d.   All of the above

True-False Statements.

1. In Brazil, as in the United States, race is virtually exclusively determined by skin color.

2.   Irish Americans in the early twentieth century were defined by more powerful White groups as a "race" that was inferior to White people.

3.   Socioeconomic status is a salient characteristic, since it is one of the first things we notice about a person.

4.   Among gender stereotypes, the stereotypes about men are more likely to be negative than those about women.

5.   Discrimination is the evaluation of a social group, and individuals within that group, based on conceptions about the group that are held despite facts that contradict it and that involve both prejudgment and misjudgment.

6.   A major vehicle for the communication of racial-ethnic attitudes to both young and old persons is the media, especially television, magazines, newspapers, and books.

7.   The median income of Black and Hispanic families has increased substantially since 1950, so that the income gap between these groups and Whites has virtually disappeared.

8.   Two social psychological theories of prejudice are the scapegoat theory and functionalism.

9.   Approximately 55 percent of Native Americans live on or near reservations.

10.   The development of slavery in the Americas was related to the development of world markets for sugar and tobacco.

11.   Latino Americans include Chicanos and Chicanas, Puerto Ricans, Cubans, and other recent Latin American immigrants to the U.S.

12.   Nearly 10 percent of the world's Jewish live in the United States, making it the second largest community of Jews in the world.

13.   In 1924, the National Origins Quota Act was passed by the U.S. This was one of the most discriminatory actions ever taken by the U.S. in the field of immigration.

14.   While de facto segregation has been virtually eliminated in the U.S. by legislation that mandates desegregation, de jure segregation, particularly in housing and education, is still evident.

15.   Malcolm X advocated a form of pluralism which demanded separate business establishments, banks, churches, and schools for Black Americans.

Short-Answer Questions.
A page reference to the relevant text material is provided in the parenthesis.

1.   Define each of the following terms and provide one example of each: ethnic group, race, minority group, and dominant group (221).

2.   Define stereotypes and discuss the significance of the salience principle. Discuss whether or not salient characteristics are culturally determined (225).

3.   Distinguish prejudice, ethnocentrism, discrimination, and racism. How do they differ? How are they similar? Provide one example of each. What is institutional racism (226)?

4.   Summarize each of the following theories of prejudice and racism: scapegoat theory, authoritarian personality, functionalism, symbolic interaction, and conflict theory (230).

66

5.   Compare and contrast assimilation and pluralism. Define segregation and the urban underclass (238).

ANSWERS TO THE MULTIPLE-CHOICE QUESTIONS.

1. B 221 An ethnic group is a social category of people who share a common culture, a common language or dialect, religion, norms, customs, and history.
2. C 223 A race is a group treated as distinct in society on the basis of certain characteristics, some of which are biological, that have been assigned social importance in society.
3. A 224 Racial formation is the process by which a group comes to be defined as a race.
4. D 224 The group that assigns a racial or ethnic group to subordinate status in society is called the dominant group and social majority.
5. D 224 In general, a racial or ethnic minority group has each of the following characteristics: it suffers prejudice and discrimination by the dominant group, membership in the group is frequently ascribed rather than achieved, and members of a minority group feel a strong sense of solidarity.
6. D 221 Italian Americans, Japanese Americans, Arab Americans, Serbians and Croatians in Bosnia, and the tribal Hutus and Tutsis in Rwanda are examples of ethnic groups.
7. C 223 The biological differences that are presumed to define different racial groups are somewhat arbitrary.
8. B 225 A stereotype is an oversimplified set of beliefs about members of a social group or social stratum that is used to categorize individuals of that group.
9. A 226 The evaluation of a social group, and individuals within that group, based on conceptions about the social group that are held despite facts that contradict it and that involve both prejudgment and misjudgment is prejudice.
10. B 227 Ethnocentrism is the belief that one's group is superior to all other groups.
11. A 227 The overt negative and unequal treatment of the members of some social group or stratum solely because of their membership in that group or stratum is discrimination.
12. C 224 A minority group is any distinct group in society that shares common group characteristics and is forced to occupy low status in society because of prejudice and discrimination.
13. A 226 The categorization of people into groups and the subsequent applications of stereotypes are based on the salience principle, which states that we categorize people on the basis of what appears initially prominent and obvious about them.
14. C 225 The principle of stereotype interchangeability holds that stereotypes, especially negative ones, are often able to be applied to different social classes, racial and ethnic groups, and gender groups.
15. B 228 The spatial separation of racial and ethnic groups into different neighborhoods is residential segregation.
16. D 229 The negative treatment and oppression of one racial or ethnic group by society's existing institutions based on the presumed inferiority of the oppressed group is institutional racism.
17. A 230 Scapegoat theory argues that, historically, members of the dominant group in the U.S. have harbored various frustrations in their desire to achieve social and economic success.
18. C 230 According to Adorno et. al., the authoritarian personality is characterized by a tendency to rigidly characterize other people, as well as tendencies to submit to authority, rigidly conform, be very intolerant of ambiguity, and be inclined to superstition.
19. B 230 The process by which a minority becomes, socially, economically, and culturally absorbed within the dominant society is assimilation.
20. D 231 All of the following statements about the interaction between Whites and minorities which will reduce prejudice is (are) TRUE, according to contact theorists. The contact must be between individuals of equal status. The contact between equals must be sustained. Social norms favoring equality must be agreed upon by the participants.
21. C 231 The gendered racism theory investigates the interaction or combined effects of race and sex in the oppression of women of color.

22.	B	233	The minority group which has the highest poverty rate in the United States is Native Americans.
23.	A	238	Persons with the assimilationist perspective believe that to overcome adversity and oppression, the minority person needs to imitate the dominant White culture as much as possible.
24.	D	239	Different groups in a society which maintain their distinctive cultures while coexisting with the dominant group characterize cultural pluralism.
25.	C	239	The spatial and social segregation of racial and ethnic groups is segregation.
26.	A	242	The refusal of Rosa Parks to relinquish her seat in the "White only" section on a segregated bus began the Montgomery Bus Boycott in 1955.
27.	B	243	Race-specific policies are those that recognize the unique status of racial groups because of the long history of discrimination and the continuing influence of institutional racism.
28.	A	244	A controversial program for change to reduce job and educational inequality is known as affirmative action.
29.	D	243	The Black power movement of the 1960s rejected assimilation and demanded self-determination and self-regulation of Black communities. Many of the leaders of the Black power movement were eliminated, through assassinations, imprisonment, or other means. The Black power movement argued that racial inequality was rooted in the institutional power that Whites and over Black Americans.
30.	D	221	Ethnic groups can develop more or less intense ethnic identification at different points in time. Ethnic identification may grow stronger when groups face prejudice or hostility from other groups. Ethnic unity can develop voluntarily or may be imposed when ethnic groups are excluded by more powerful groups from certain residential areas, occupations, or social clubs.

ANSWERS TO THE TRUE-FALSE STATEMENTS.

1.	F	222	In Brazil, one's race is in part defined by one's social class.
2.	T	223	Irish Americans in the early twentieth century were defined by more powerful White groups as a "race" that was inferior to White people.
3.	F	225	Race is a salient characteristic, since it is one of the first things we notice about a person.
4.	F	225	Among gender stereotypes, the stereotypes about women are more likely to be negative than those about men.
5.	F	226	Prejudice is the evaluation of a social group, and individuals within that group, based on conceptions about the group that are held despite facts that contradict it and that involve both prejudgment and misjudgment.
6.	T	227	A major vehicle for the communication of racial-ethnic attitudes to both young and old persons is the media, especially television, magazines, newspapers, and books.
7.	F	228	The median income of Black and Hispanic families has increased somewhat since 1950, but the income gap between these groups and Whites has remained virtually unchanged since 1967.
8.	F	230	Two social psychological theories of prejudice are the scapegoat theory and the theory of the authoritarian personality.
9.	T	233	Approximately 55 percent of Native Americans live on or near reservations.
10.	T	233	The development of slavery in the Americas was related to the development of world markets for sugar and tobacco.
11.	T	233	Latino Americans include Chicanos and Chicanas, Puerto Ricans, Cubans, and other recent Latin American immigrants to the U.S.
12.	F	238	More than 40 percent of the world's Jewish live in the United States, making it the largest community of Jews in the world.
13.	T	238	In 1924, the National Origins Quota Act was passed by the U.S. This was one of the most discriminatory actions ever taken by the U.S. in the field of immigration.

14.   F   239   While de jure segregation has been virtually eliminated in the U.S. by legislation that mandates desegregation, de facto segregation, particularly in housing and education, is still evident.

15.   T   243   Malcolm X advocated a form of pluralism which demanded separate business establishments, banks, churches, and schools for Black Americans.

Chapter Ten

SEX AND GENDER

Multiple-Choice statements. Select the best response.

1. _____ refers to the biological identity as male or female.
    a.   Gender
    b.   Sexual identity
    c.   Gendered identity
    d.   Sex

2. The socially learned expectations associated with members of each sex are:
    a.   gender
    b.   sexual status
    c.   gender status
    d.   sex

3. The term _____ refers to expectations that attribute complex social phenomena to physical characteristics.
    a.   hermaphroditism
    b.   biological determinism
    c.   gender socialization
    d.   liberal feminism

4. The condition produced when irregularities in chromosome formation or fetal differentiation produce persons with mixed biological sexual characteristics is:
    a.   hermaphroditism
    b.   mutation
    c.   bisexuality
    d.   transsexuality

5. _____ teach us what is appropriate sexual behavior for a person of our gender.
    a.   Sex roles
    b.   The media
    c.   Sexual scripts
    d.   Peer groups

6. Through _____, men and women learn the expectations associated with their sex.
    a.   sexual scripts
    b.   gender socialization
    c.   the media
    d.   religious institutions

7. The definition of oneself as a woman or a man is one's:
    a.   self-concept
    b.   self-image
    c.   ego
    d.   gender identity

8. Which of the following are sources of gender socialization?
    a.   popular culture
    b.   schools
    c.   religion
    d.   all of the above

9. _____ is how individuals experience sexual arousal and pleasure.
   a. Sexuality
   b. Sexual orientation
   c. Pornography
   d. None of the above

10. The fear and hatred of homosexuality is:
    a. homophobia
    b. homosexual aversion
    c. homosexual animosity
    d. homosexual revulsion

11. _____ are the total pattern of gender relations, including stereotypical expectations, interpersonal relationships, and the different placement of men and women in social, economic, and political hierarchies of institutions.
    a. Gender discrimination
    b. Gender prejudice
    c. Gendered institutions
    d. Gendered societies

12. The institutionalization of heterosexuality as the only socially legitimate sexual orientation is:
    a. homophobia
    b. heterosexism
    c. morally right
    d. all of the above

13. The hierarchical distribution of social and economic resources according to gender is:
    a. the gendered world of work
    b. the glass ceiling
    c. gendered segregation
    d. gender stratification

14. Based on comparative research, women are more nearly equal to men in societies characterized by:
    a. Women have access to education.
    b. Women make virtually all contributions to household responsibilities, such as housework and child care.
    c. Work is highly segregated by sex.
    d. All of the above

15. _____ is an ideology, but it is also a set of institutional practices and beliefs through which women are controlled because of the significance given to differences between the sexes.
    a. Feminism
    b. The sexual revolution
    c. Sexism
    d. Socialist feminism

16. The term _____ refers to a society or group in which men have power over women.
    a. gender inequality
    b. patriarchy
    c. patrilocal
    d. universal

17. The _____ is the percentage of those in a given category who are employed part time or full time.
    a. rate of employment
    b. employment ratio
    c. labor force participation rate
    d. a and b

18. Gender differences in wages are explained by _____ as the result of differences in the individual characteristics that workers bring to jobs.
    a. human capital theory
    b. dual labor market theory
    c. conflict theory
    d. feminism

19. The theory which contends that women and men earn different amounts because they tend to work in different segments of the labor market is:
    a. human capital theory
    b. dual labor market theory
    c. conflict theory
    d. feminism

20. The term _____ refers to the distribution of men and women in different jobs in the labor force.
    a. sexist segregation
    b. patriarchal promotion
    c. glass ceiling
    d. gender segregation

21. _____ refers to practices that single out some groups for different and unequal treatment.
    a. Prejudice
    b. Sexism
    c. Discrimination
    d. Institutional sexism

22. Which of the following are cited as reasons for gender segregation?
    a. Women and men are socialized differently and choose to enter different fields.
    b. Structural obstacles discourage women from entering male-dominated jobs and from advancing once they are employed.
    c. Another structural barrier to the advancement of women is women's family responsibilities.
    d. All of the above.

23. _____ theory argues that men fill instrumental roles in society, whereas women fill expressive roles, and this arrangement benefits society.
    a. Conflict
    b. Functionalist
    c. Symbolic interaction
    d. Feminist

24. A theoretical perspective on gender that interprets gender as something that is accomplished through the ongoing social interactions people have with one another is:
    a. doing gender
    b. functionalism
    c. feminism
    d. conflict theory

25. The term _____ refers to analyses that seek to understand the position of women in society for the purposes of bringing about liberating social changes.
    a. liberation theory
    b. gender equity theory
    c. feminist theory
    d. symbolic interaction theory

26. _____ feminism interprets patriarchy as the primary cause of women's oppression and believes that change cannot come about through the existing system, since it is controlled and dominated by men.
    a. Socialist
    b. Multiracial
    c. Liberal
    d. Radical

27. Which of the following statements about public attitudes toward gender roles is (are) TRUE?
    a. Approximately one-half of people disapprove of women being employed while they have young children.
    b. Approximately three-quarters of men believe that it is best for men to hold the provider role.
    c. Younger men and single men are more egalitarian than older, married men.
    d. All of the above

28. The term _____ refers to the widespread changes in men's and women's roles and a greater public acceptance of sexuality as a normal part of social development.
    a. gender wars
    b. sexual revolution
    c. decline in morality
    d. all of the above

29. _____ allows educational institutions to spend more money on male athletes if they outnumber female athletes, but it also stipulates that the number of males and females should be roughly proportional to their representation in the student body.
    a. Title IX
    b. The Civil rights Act of 1964
    c. Title VII
    d. Affirmative action

30. _____ is the principle of paying women and men equivalent wages for jobs involving similar levels of skill.
    a. Affirmative action
    b. Gender segregation
    c. Comparable worth
    d. Gender stratification

True-False Statements.

1. Generally, men develop a more competitive orientation than women, particularly when competition means winning over an opponent.

2. Gender expectations for Mexican and Puerto Rican women are less traditional in the older generation and older women are more likely to be employed than younger women.

3. In Sweden, where there is a relatively high degree of gender equality, the participation of both men and women in the workforce and the household is promoted by government policies.

4. Homophobia plays an important role in gender socialization because it encourages stricter conformity to traditional expectations, especially for men and young boys.

5. Younger women describe themselves as more assertive, competent, and effective than older women do.

6. Changes in family patterns in contemporary society mean that more men are the sole supporters of their dependents.

7. According to dual labor market theory, employment in the secondary market is characterized by good wages, stable jobs, opportunities for advancement, fringe benefits, and due process.

8. Only a small proportion of women work in occupations traditionally thought to be men's jobs.

9. Worldwide, women work as much or more than men and receive 30 to 40 percent less pay.

10. Socialist feminism argues that inequality originates in traditions of the past that pose barriers to women's advancement. It emphasizes individual rights and equal opportunities as the basis for social justice and social reform.

11. Comparable worth goes beyond the concept of equal pay for equal work by creating job evaluation systems that assess the degree of similarity between different kinds of jobs.

12. Multiracial feminism examines the interactive influence of gender, race, and class, showing how race, class, and gender together shape the experiences of all women and men.

13. Symbolic interaction theorists see women as disadvantaged by power inequities between women and men that are built into the social structure.

14. Boys in all-boy groups tend to give polite directives, express agreement with one another, and take turns speaking.

15. There can be substantial differences in the construction of gender across social classes or subcultures within a single society.

Short-Answer Questions.
A page reference to the relevant text material is provided in the parenthesis.

1. Define and discuss each of the following terms: sex, gender, biological determinism, hermaphroditism, and transgendered persons (248).

2. List and discuss the four social and cultural characteristics of human sexuality which were discussed in the textbook (251).

3. List and discuss the five sources of gender socialization which were discussed in the textbook. Which two do you believe are the most important? Why (253)?

4. List and discuss the six characteristics of societies in which women are more nearly equal to men. Are any of these characteristics evident in the United States (260)?

5. Compare and contrast the following theories of gender differences in wages: human capital theory, dual labor market theory, gender segregation, and overt discrimination (263).

6. Compare and contrast feminism, liberal feminism, socialist feminism, radical feminism, and multiracial feminism. Do any of these perspectives reflect your beliefs and values about gender issues? If so, which one seems most appropriate to you and why (268)?

74

1.	D	248	Sex refers to the biological identity as male or female.
2.	A	248	The socially learned expectations associated with members of each sex are gender.
3.	B	249	The term biological determinism refers to expectations that attribute complex social phenomena to physical characteristics.
4.	A	250	The condition produced when irregularities in chromosome formation or fetal differentiation produce persons with mixed biological sexual characteristics is hermaphroditism.
5.	C	251	Sexual scripts teach us what is appropriate sexual behavior for a person of our gender.
6.	B	252	Through gender socialization, men and women learn the expectations associated with their sex.
7.	D	252	The definition of oneself as a woman or a man is one's gender identity.
8.	D	253	Sources of gender socialization include popular culture, schools, and religion.
9.	B	257	Sexual orientation is how individuals experience sexual arousal and pleasure.
10.	A	258	The fear and hatred of homosexuality is homophobia.
11.	C	259	Gendered institutions are the total pattern of gender relations, including stereotypical expectations, interpersonal relationships, and the different placement of men and women in social, economic, and political hierarchies of institutions.
12.	B	258	The institutionalization of heterosexuality as the only socially legitimate sexual orientation is heterosexism.
13.	D	260	The hierarchical distribution of social and economic resources according to gender is gender stratification.
14.	A	260	Based on comparative research, women are more nearly equal to men in societies characterized by women having access to education.
15.	C	260	Sexism is an ideology, but it is also a set of institutional practices and beliefs through which women are controlled because of the significance given to differences between the sexes.
16.	B	261	The term patriarchy refers to a society or group in which men have power over women.
17.	C	262	The labor force participation rate is the percentage of those in a given category who are employed part time or full time.
18.	A	263	Gender differences in wages are explained by human capital theory as the result of differences in the individual characteristics that workers bring to jobs.
19.	B	263	The theory which contends that women and men earn different amounts because they tend to work in different segments of the labor market is dual labor market theory.
20.	D	264	The term gender segregation refers to the distribution of men and women in different jobs in the labor force.
21.	C	264	Discrimination refers to practices that single out some groups for different and unequal treatment.
22.	D	266	Women and men are socialized differently and choose to enter different fields. Structural obstacles discourage women from entering male-dominated jobs and from advancing once they are employed. Another structural barrier to the advancement of women is women's family responsibilities.
23.	B	268	Functionalist theory argues that men fill instrumental roles in society, whereas women fill expressive roles, and this arrangement benefits society.
24.	A	268	A theoretical perspective on gender that interprets gender as something that is accomplished through the ongoing social interactions people have with one another is doing gender.
25.	C	268	The term feminist theory refers to analyses that seek to understand the position of women in society for the purposes of bringing about liberating social changes.
26.	D	269	Radical feminism interprets patriarchy as the primary cause of women's oppression and believes that change cannot come about through the existing system, since it is controlled and dominated by men.
27.	C	270	Younger men and single men are more egalitarian than older, married men.
28.	B	270	The term sexual revolution refers to the widespread changes in men's and women's

roles and a greater public acceptance of sexuality as a normal part of social development.

29.   A   272   Title IX allows educational institutions to spend more money on male athletes if they outnumber female athletes, but it also stipulates that the number of males and females should be roughly proportional to their representation in the student body.

30.   C   273   Comparable worth is the principle of paying women and men equivalent wages for jobs involving similar levels of skill.

ANSWERS TO THE TRUE-FALSE STATEMENTS.

1.   T   252   Generally, men develop a more competitive orientation than women, particularly when competition means winning over an opponent.

2.   F   253   Gender expectations for Mexican and Puerto Rican women are more traditional in the older generation and older women are less likely to be employed than younger women.

3.   T   260   In Sweden, where there is a relatively high degree of gender equality, the participation of both men and women in the workforce and the household is promoted by government policies.

4.   T   258   Homophobia plays an important role in gender socialization because it encourages stricter conformity to traditional expectations, especially for men and young boys.

5.   F   255   Older women describe themselves as more assertive, competent, and effective than younger women do.

6.   F   262   Changes in family patterns in contemporary society mean that more women are the sole supporters of their dependents.

7.   F   263   According to dual labor market theory, employment in the primary market is characterized by good wages, stable jobs, opportunities for advancement, fringe benefits, and due process.

8.   T   265   Only a small proportion of women work in occupations traditionally thought to be men's jobs.

9.   T   267   Worldwide, women work as much or more than men and receive 30 to 40 percent less pay.

10.   F   269   Liberal feminism argues that inequality originates in traditions of the past that pose barriers to women's advancement. It emphasizes individual rights and equal opportunities as the basis for social justice and social reform.

11.   T   273   Comparable worth goes beyond the concept of equal pay for equal work by creating job evaluation systems that assess the degree of similarity between different kinds of jobs.

12.   T   269   Multiracial feminism examines the interactive influence of gender, race, and class, showing how race, class, and gender together shape the experiences of all women and men.

13.   F   268   Conflict theorists see women as disadvantaged by power inequities between women and men that are built into the social structure.

14.   F   252   Girls in all-girl groups tend to give polite directives, express agreement with one another, and take turns speaking.

15.   T   249   There can be substantial differences in the construction of gender across social classes or subcultures within a single society.

Chapter Eleven

FAMILIES

Multiple-Choice Questions. Select the best response.

1. A primary group of people, usually related by ancestry, marriage, or adoption, who form a cooperative economic unit to care for any offspring and who are committed to maintaining the group over time is a(n):
    a. kinship group
    b. family
    c. nuclear family
    d. extended family

2. A(n) _____ is the pattern of relationships that define people's family relationships to one another.
    a. kinship system
    b. matriarchal system
    c. patriarchal system
    d. egalitarian system

3. _____ is the practice of men and women having multiple marriage partners.
    a. Polyandry
    b. Monogamy
    c. Polygyny
    d. Polygamy

4. The practice of selecting mates from one's own group is:
    a. exogamy
    b. endogamy
    c. homogamy
    d. heterogamy

5. _____ prohibited marriage between various groups, including between Whites and African Americans and between Whites and Chinese, Japanese, Filipinos, Hawaiians, Hindus, and Native Americans.
    a. Interbreeding prohibitions
    b. Miscegenation laws
    c. Anti-miscegenation laws
    d. Anti-amalgamation laws

6. In _____ systems, family lineage or ancestry is traced through the father of the family.
    a. patrilineal
    b. matrilineal
    c. matrilocal
    d. neolocal

7. In _____ kinship systems, descent is traced through both the father and mother.
    a. dual-descent
    b. egalitarian
    c. symmetrical
    d. bilateral

8. In _____ systems, a women continues to live with her family of origin and her husband resides with his wife and her family, although he does not give up membership in his own group.
    a. maternal
    b. bilateral
    c. matrilocal
    d. patrilocal

9. _____ societies are those where men and women share power equally.
    a. Egalitarian
    b. Democratic
    c. Western
    d. All of the above

10. _____ families are those in which a large number of related kin in addition to parents and children live together in the same household.
    a. Nuclear
    b. Extended
    c. Multi-generational
    d. Blended

11. According to sociologists, African American women, who historically have been likely to be employed outside of their household, have utilized _____ to assist bloodmothers by sharing mothering responsibilities.
    a. surrogate mothers
    b. babysitters
    c. grandmothers and aunts
    d. othermothers

12. According to functionalist theorists, which of the following statements is (are) TRUE?
    a. Families exist to socialize the young, regulate sexual activity and procreation, provide physical care for family members, and give psychological support and emotional security to individuals.
    b. When societies experience disruption and change, institutions such as the family become disorganized, which weakens the consensus around which they have formed.
    c. Over time, other social institutions, such as schools, have begun to take on some of the functions originally performed solely by the family.
    d. All of the above

13. Which of the following statements about families in the United States is (are) TRUE?
    a. The majority of families, approximately 63 percent, fit the so-called family ideal, with the family as a nuclear unit with a father as head and two or three children.
    b. There are fewer births in families today than in the past and they are spaced over a longer period of time.
    c. Death, once the major cause of early family disruption, has been replaced by divorce.
    d. All of the above

14. The causes of the growing number of women heading their own households in the United States include:
    a. the high rate of pregnancy among unmarried teens
    b. the high rate of spousal death due to violence
    c. the decline in the morality of U.S. teens
    d. all of the above

15. Individuals who perform multiple tasks at the same time, find it difficult to manage their time or catch up with chores, and believe they don't have enough tome for their children or partners are experiencing:
    a. neurosis
    b. social speedup
    c. social insecurity
    d. social acceleration

16. The term _____ refers to the work performed at home by women who work all day in paid employment.
    a. second shift
    b. double burden
    c. domestic duties
    d. mother's mandate

17. Which of the following statements about divorce is (are) TRUE?
    a. First marriages are more likely to end in divorce than second marriages.
    b. Divorce is more likely for persons who delay marriage until their 30s.
    c. For most groups, the divorce rate is higher among low-income couples, which reflects the strains that financial problems put on marriages.
    d. a and b

18. Which of the following statements about partner abuse is (are) TRUE?
    a. The American Medical Association has estimated that one in three women will be physically assaulted by their husbands at some time in their married life.
    b. Studies show that at least 10 percent of married women will be raped by their husbands.
    c. Violence is more prevalent in gay and lesbian relationships than in heterosexual relationships.
    d. a and b

19. The proportion of old people is increasing dramatically in the U.S. This process is referred to as the:
    a. aging of America
    b. graying of America
    c. maturing of America
    d. all of the above

20. The question of whether one age group or generation is unfairly taxed to support the needs and interests of another generation is termed:
    a. age cohort equity
    b. generational fairness
    c. generational equity
    d. the needs of the young vs. the needs of the old

21. The federal legislation, passed in 1993, which requires employers to grant employees a total of twelve weeks of unpaid leave to care for newborns, adopted children, or other family members with a serious health condition, is:
    a. The Family and Medical Leave Act (FMLA)
    b. Title IX
    c. The Parents and Illness Act (PIA)
    d. Title VII

22. The marriage practice of a sexually exclusive marriage with one spouse at a time, which is the most common practice in the U.S. and other Western industrialized nations, is:
    a. polygamy
    b. monogamy
    c. polygyny
    d. monogyny

23. The practice of selecting mates from outside one's group, based on religion, territory, racial identity, etc., is:
    a. intergamy
    b. endogamy
    c. intragamy
    d. exogamy

24. _____ kinship systems are those in which ancestry is traced through the mother.
    a. Patrilineal
    b. Matridescent
    c. Matrilineal
    d. Patridescent

25. The practice of married couples establishing their own residence is:
    a. matrilocal residence
    b. patrilocal residence
    c. neolocal residence
    d. most common in horticultural and agricultural societies

26. A(n) _____ is a society or group where men have power over women.
    a. patriarchy
    b. matriarchy
    c. matrilocal unit
    d. endogamous society

27. The _____ family is one where a married couple resides together with their children.
    a. extended
    b. consanguine
    c. exogamous
    d. nuclear

28. The _____ perspective views families as the units through which the privileges, as well as the disadvantages, of race, class, and gender are acquired.
    a. functionalist
    b. conflict
    c. symbolic interaction
    d. differential association

29. The arrangement that typically arises when work requires one partner in a dual-career couple to reside in a different city much of the time is:
    a. commuter marriage
    b. dual residence marriage
    c. limited to professional couples
    d. much less common than typically imagined

30. Young people who return home in their twenties when they would normally be expected to live independently are known as:
    a. Generation Z
    b. psychotics
    c. the boomerang generation
    d. the socially displaced generation

True-False Statements.

1. Polygyny, or the practice of a woman having more than one husband, is an extremely rare custom.

80

2. Many sociologists characterize modern marriage as serial monogamy, in which an individual, over the course of a lifetime, may have more than one marriage, but maintains only one spouse at a time.

3. Among Native American groups, family ancestry is often traced through paternal descent.

4. The origin of the nuclear family in Western society is tied to industrialization.

5. Feminists have criticized the functionalist theory of families for being based on stereotypes about men's and women's roles and on proscriptions about what family life was supposed to be, not on empirically accurate analyses of the sociology of the family.

6. Most men, as a result of court-mandated child-support and alimony payments, experience a substantial decline in their income in the year following a divorce.

7. The rate of pregnancy among both White and Black teenagers, married and unmarried, is higher today than it was in 1960.

8. Among married-couple families, one of the greatest changes has been the increased participation of women in the paid labor force.

9. In the U.S., approximately 15 percent of marriages involve stepchildren.

10. In the U.S., single people, including those never married and those widowed and divorced, constitute 19 percent of the population over the age of 18, which constitutes a decrease from earlier years.

11. The United States leads the world not only in the number of people who marry, but also in the number of people who divorce.

12. Sociological analysis of violence in the family have led to the conclusion that women's relative powerlessness in the family is at the root of high rates of violence against women.

13. Most of the care of older people in the U.S. is provided informally by families, mostly by women.

14. In recent years, the percentage of teens using birth control, especially condom use, has decreased.

15. The proportion of public funds directed to the elderly has decreased while resources to other groups, such as children and the poor, have increased.

Short-Answer Questions.
A page reference to the relevant text material is provided in the parenthesis.

1. Define each of the following terms: family, kinship system, polygamy, polygyny, polyandry, and monogamy (278).

2. Define exogamy, endogamy, and anti-miscegenation laws. Discuss what role each of these expectations have in the U.S. today (279).

3. Compare and contrast extended families and nuclear families. Discuss the role played by industrialization in the development of the nuclear family (280).

4. Summarize, compare, and contrast each of the following theories of families: functionalist, conflict, symbolic interaction, and feminist theory (282).

5. Briefly discuss each of the following family structures in the U.S.: female-headed households, married-couple families, stepfamilies, and gay and lesbians households (285).

6.   Briefly discuss each of the following social problems which affect families in the U.S.: partner violence, child abuse, incest, elder care, and elder abuse.

ANSWERS TO THE MULTIPLE-CHOICE QUESTIONS.

1.   B   278   A primary group of people, usually related by ancestry, marriage, or adoption, who form a cooperative economic unit to care for any offspring and who are committed to maintaining the group over time is a family.

2.   A   278   A kinship system is the pattern of relationships that define people's family relationships to one another.

3.   D   278   Polygamy is the practice of men and women having multiple marriage partners.

4.   B   279   The practice of selecting mates from one's own group is endogamy.

5.   C   279   Anti-miscegenation laws prohibited marriage between various groups, including between Whites and African Americans and between Whites and Chinese, Japanese, Filipinos, Hawaiians, Hindus, and Native Americans.

6.   A   270   In patrilineal systems, family lineage or ancestry is traced through the father of the family.

7.   D   279   In bilateral kinship systems, descent is traced through both the father and mother.

8.   C   279   In matrilocal systems, a women continues to live with her family of origin and her husband resides with his wife and her family, although he does not give up membership in his own group.

9.   A   280   Egalitarian societies are those where men and women share power equally.

10.   B   280   Extended families are those in which a large number of related kin in addition to parents and children live together in the same household.

11.   D   280   According to sociologists, African American women, who historically have been likely to be employed outside of their household, have utilized othermothers to assist bloodmothers by sharing mothering responsibilities.

12.   D   282   According to functionalist theorists, families exist to socialize the young, regulate sexual activity and procreation, provide physical care for family members, and give psychological support and emotional security to individuals. When societies experience disruption and change, institutions such as the family become disorganized, which weakens the consensus around which they have formed. Over time, other social institutions, such as schools, have begun to take on some of the functions originally performed solely by the family.

13.   C   284   Death, once the major cause of early family disruption, has been replaced by divorce.

14.   A   285   The causes of the growing number of women heading their own households in the United States include the high rate of pregnancy among unmarried teens.

15.   B   291   Individuals who perform multiple tasks at the same time, find it difficult to manage their time or catch up with chores, and believe they don't have enough tome for their children or partners are experiencing social speedup.

16.   A   291   The term second shift refers to the work performed at home by women who work all day in paid employment.

17.   C   292   For most groups, the divorce rate is higher among low-income couples, which reflects the strains that financial problems put on marriages.

18.   D   294   The American Medical Association has estimated that one in three women will be physically assaulted by their husbands at some time in their married life. Studies show that at least 10 percent of married women will be raped by their husbands.

19.   B   298   The proportion of old people is increasing dramatically in the U.S. This process is referred to as the graying of America.

20.   C   299   The question of whether one age group or generation is unfairly taxed to support the needs and interests of another generation is termed generational equity.

21.   A   300   The federal legislation, passed in 1993, which requires employers to grant employees a total of twelve weeks of unpaid leave to care for newborns, adopted children, or other family members with a serious health condition, is The Family and Medical Leave Act (FMLA).

22.	B	278	The marriage practice of a sexually exclusive marriage with one spouse at a time, which is the most common practice in the U.S. and other Western industrialized nations, is monogamy.
23.	D	279	The practice of selecting mates from outside one's group, based on religion, territory, racial identity, etc., is exogamy.
24.	C	279	Matrilineal kinship systems are those in which ancestry is traced through the mother.
25.	C	279	The practice of married couples establishing their own residence is neolocal residence.
26.	A	279	A patriarchy is a society or group where men have power over women.
27.	D	280	The nuclear family is one where a married couple resides together with their children.
28.	B	283	The conflict perspective views families as the units through which the privileges, as well as the disadvantages, of race, class, and gender are acquired.
29.	A	287	The arrangement that typically arises when work requires one partner in a dual-career couple to reside in a different city much of the time is commuter marriage.
30.	C	290	Young people who return home in their twenties when they would normally be expected to live independently are known as the boomerang generation.

ANSWERS TO THE TRUE-FALSE STATEMENTS.

1.	F	278	Polyandry, or the practice of a woman having more than one husband, is an extremely rare custom.
2.	T	278	Many sociologists characterize modern marriage as serial monogamy, in which an individual, over the course of a lifetime, may have more than one marriage, but maintains only one spouse at a time.
3.	F	279	Among Native American groups, family ancestry is often traced through maternal descent.
4.	T	280	The origin of the nuclear family in Western society is tied to industrialization.
5.	T	283	Feminists have criticized the functionalist theory of families for being based on stereotypes about men's and women's roles and on proscriptions about what family life was supposed to be, not on empirically accurate analyses of the sociology of the family.
6.	F	285	Most women experience a substantial decline in their income in the year following a divorce.
7.	F	285	The rate of pregnancy among both White and Black teenagers, married and unmarried, is lower today than it was in 1960.
8.	T	286	Among married-couple families, one of the greatest changes has been the increased participation of women in the paid labor force.
9.	F	287	In the U.S., approximately 40 percent of marriages involve stepchildren.
10.	F	289	In the U.S., single people, including those never married and those widowed and divorced, constitute 42 percent of the population over the age of 18, which constitutes a increase from earlier years.
11.	T	292	The United States leads the world not only in the number of people who marry, but also in the number of people who divorce.
12.	T	294	Sociological analysis of violence in the family have led to the conclusion that women's relative powerlessness in the family is at the root of high rates of violence against women.
13.	T	296	Most of the care of older people in the U.S. is provided informally by families, mostly by women.
14.	F	297	In recent years, the percentage of teens using birth control, especially condom use, has increased.
15.	F	299	The proportion of public funds directed to the elderly has increased while resources to other groups, such as children and the poor, have decreased.

Chapter Twelve

EDUCATION AND WORK

Multiple-Choice Statements. Select the best response.

1. Which of the following is (are) considered to be among the functions of education?
    a. Socialization is brought about as the cultural heritage is passed on from one generation to another.
    b. Occupational training, which is particularly important in an industrialized society like the United States, occurs.
    c. Social control, largely be keeping young people off the streets and out of trouble, is achieved.
    d. All of the above

2. Which of the following statements is (are) criticisms of standardized tests?
    a. Standardized tests tend to measure only limited ranges of ability, while ignoring other cognitive endowments, such as creativity.
    b. Standardized tests evidence cultural bias and gender bias.
    c. IQ tests and SATs do not predict school performance very well even for Whites.
    d. All of the above

3. _____ refers to the extent to which standardized tests accurately predict later college grades.
    a. Predictive reliability
    b. Predictive validity
    c. Predictive accuracy
    d. Predictive ratio

4. Herrnstein and Murray, in *The Bell Curve*, argue that:
    a. intelligence is inherited
    b. intelligence is primarily determined by one's social and educational environment
    c. there is an overrepresentation of persons with genes for high intelligence in the lower classes
    d. a and c

5. The process, which is commonly found in U.S. schools, of separating students on the basis of their performance on some measure of cognitive ability is:
    a. tracking
    b. segregation
    c. ability grouping
    d. a and c

6. The effect of teacher expectations on a student's performance, independent of the student's actual ability, is the _____ effect.
    a. teacher expectancy
    b. labeling
    c. quality of the teacher-student relationship
    d. self-fulfilling prophecy

7. The effect of teacher expectations on a student's actual performance, independent of the student's actual ability, is the _____ effect.
    a. teacher expectancy
    b. labeling
    c. quality of the teacher-student relationship
    d. self-fulfilling prophecy

8.   Which of the following statements about schooling and gender is (are) TRUE?
      a.   Standardized tests in math tend to overpredict women's actual grades in mathematics.
      b.   Teachers tend to treat Black women and White women differently.
      c.   As girls and boys approach adolescence, their self-esteem tends to drop, with the erosion of self-esteem occurring more quickly among boys than girls.
      d.   In general, teachers pay less attention to boys and men.

9.   The _____ of a society is the system by which goods and services are produced, distributed, and consumed.
      a.   economy
      b.   financial institution
      c.   stock market
      d.   production market

10.   _____ is a broad term, meant to encompass a wide range of economic activities now common in the labor market, including banking and finance, retail sales, hotel and restaurant work, and healthcare.
      a.   The national economy
      b.   The global economy
      c.   Service industry
      d.   Economic interdependence

11.   An economic system based on the principles of market competition, private property, and the pursuit of profit is:
      a.   communism
      b.   Marxism
      c.   socialism
      d.   capitalism

12.   In pure _____, industry is not the private property of owners. Rather, the state is the sole owner of the systems of production.
      a.   capitalism
      b.   communism
      c.   industrialization
      d.   postindustrialization

13.   The concept of the _____ economy acknowledges that all dimensions of the economy now cross national borders, including investment, production, management, markets, labor, information, and technology.
      a.   global
      b.   international
      c.   20th Century
      d.   transnational

14.   The fear and hatred of foreigners is:
      a.   immigrantphobia
      b.   xenophobia
      c.   foreignphobia
      d.   all of the above

15.   The term _____ refers to the contemporary transformations in the basic structure of work that are permanently altering the workplace.
      a.   dual labor market
      b.   global economy
      c.   automation
      d.   economic restructuring

16.   The term _____ refers to the transition from a predominantly goods-producing economy to one based on the provision of services.
  a.   economic restructuring
  b.   global economy
  c.   deindustrialization
  d.   economic transformation

17.   The process by which human labor is replaced by machines:
  a.   is known as automation
  b.   eliminates many repetitive and tiresome tasks
  c.   makes rapid communication and access to information possible
  d.   all of the above

18.   A side effect of automation and technological progress in which the level of skill required to perform certain jobs declines over time is:
  a.   deskilling
  b.   alienation
  c.   detracking
  d.   b and c

19.   Sociologists define _____ as productive human activity that creates something of value, either goods or services.
  a.   cognition
  b.   work
  c.   creativity
  d.   manual labor

20.   Work that is specifically intended to produce a desired state of mind in a client is:
  a.   therapy
  b.   psychoanalysis
  c.   emotional labor
  d.   the major component of the service economy

21.   _____ theorists view the transformations that are taking place in the workplace as the result of inherent tensions in the social systems, tensions that arise from the power differences between groups vying for social and economic resources.
  a.   Conflict
  b.   Functionalist
  c.   Symbolic interaction
  d.   Differential association

22.   The feeling of powerlessness and separation from society is:
  a.   psychosis
  b.   alienation
  c.   pathology
  d.   xenophobia

23. Which of the following statements about trends in who works is (are) TRUE?
   a. One of the most dramatic changes in the labor force since World War II has been the number of women employed.
   b. The percentage of employed Black and White women has converged in recent years, so that both are now equally likely to be employed.
   c. The Family and Medical Leave Act of 1993 has forced companies to write more progressive policies for family and medical leaves for their employees, although studies show that few workers are able to take advantage of this policy, because they cannot afford the time without pay.
   d. All of the above

24. The percentage of those people who are not working but are officially defined as looking for work comprise the:
   a. lower class
   b. unemployment rate
   c. underemployment rate
   d. underclass

25. _____ views the labor market as comprising two major segments: the primary labor market and the secondary labor market.
   a. Capitalism
   b. Symbolic interactionism
   c. Dual labor market theory
   d. Socialism

26. Many service jobs, such as waiting tables, nonunionized assembly work, and domestic work, are in the:
   a. secondary labor market
   b. primary labor market
   c. tertiary labor market
   d. underclass

27. _____ refers to the invisible barriers which prevent women and minorities from substantial advancement in corporate bureaucracies.
   a. The glass ceiling
   b. Racial discrimination
   c. Gender discrimination
   d. All of the above

28. _____ is defined as unwanted physical or verbal sexual behavior that occurs in the context of a relationship of unequal power and that is experienced as a threat to the victim's job or educational activities.
   a. Hostile environment
   b. Sexual aggression
   c. Lewd and lascivious behavior
   d. Sexual harassment

29. Which of the following statements about the employment of persons with disabilities is (are) TRUE?
   a. The Americans with Disabilities Act of 1973 protects disabled people from discrimination in employment and stipulates that employers and other providers, such as schools and public transportation systems, must provide "reasonable accommodation" for disabled persons.
   b. The law prohibits employers with fifteen or more employees from discriminating against either job applicants who are disabled or current employees who become disabled.
   c. Disabled people report that they are often ignored and treated as if they are invisible in the workplace.
   d. All of the above.

30. _____ is the perceived social value of an occupation in the eyes of the general public.
    a. Employment prestige
    b. Occupational prestige
    c. Occupational status
    d. Occupational worth

True-False Statements.

1. Educational until the age of 16 has been mandated throughout the U.S. since the late 1700s.

2. In the general population, there is a strong correlation between formal education and occupation, although the relationship is not perfect.

3. In the U.S., students from lower-class families have lower average scores on exams such as the Scholastic Assessment Test (SAT).

4. In general, Whites tend to score higher on IQ tests and SATs than minorities, women score higher than men, and the higher a person's social class, the higher the test score.

5. The detracking movement is based on the eblief that including students of varying cognitive abilities is more beneficial to students than tracking, especially for students in junior high and high schools.

6. When teachers have high expectations for students, they call on them more, praise them more often, and interact with them more frequently.

7. While industrialized societies are primarily organized around the production of goods, postindustrialized societies are organized around the provision of services.

8. Within socialist societies, stockholders own corporations or a share of the corporations' wealth.

9. With the new international division of labor, assembly of goods is primarily done in the U.S., Japan, Germany, and other major world powers.

10. Women and racial minorities are expected to comprise nearly 10 percent of the labor force by the year 2005.

11. In a labor market experiencing deindustrialization, there is job growth in professional and administrative positions with higher educational requirements and in some manufacturing jobs that require specific technological training.

12. The group experiencing the greatest unemployment in the U.S. currently is African Americans.

13. Recent Supreme Court cases have upheld that same-sex harassment also falls under federal legislation, as does harassment directed by women against men.

14. Jobs that employ mostly men are lower in prestige than those that employ more women.

15. The labor performed by racial minority groups has often been the lowest paid, least prestigious, and most arduous work.

Short-Answer Questions.
A page reference to the relevant text material is provided in the parenthesis.

1. List and discuss the three functions of education, according to functionalist theorists (306).

2.　　　List and discuss the three major criticisms of standardized tests, such as IQ tests and SATs (309).

3.　　　Summarize the principal arguments about human intelligence presented in *The Bell Curve*. List and discuss the three principal criticisms of this work which were discussed in the textbook (310).

4.　　　Define each of the following terms: tracking, detracking, labeling effect, teacher expectancy effect, and self-fulfilling prophecy (311).

5.　　　List and discuss the seven characteristics of education and gender identified by research and presented in the textbook. Discuss whether or not this profile of the U.S. educational system is consistent with your experience. Why or why not (314)?

6.　　　Compare and contrast each of the following economic systems: capitalism, socialism, and communism. Discuss the following terms which are related to economic changes: economic restructuring, xenophobia, deindustrialization, and technological change (315).

7.　　　Compare and contrast the following theoretical perspectives of work: functionalism, conflict, and symbolic interaction (321).

ANSWERS TO THE MULTIPLE-CHOICE QUESTIONS.

1.	D	306	Socialization is brought about as the cultural heritage is passed on from one generation to another. Occupational training, which is particularly important in an industrialized society like the United States, occurs. Social control, largely be keeping young people off the streets and out of trouble, is achieved.
2.	D	309	Standardized tests tend to measure only limited ranges of ability, while ignoring other cognitive endowments, such as creativity. Standardized tests evidence cultural bias and gender bias. IQ tests and SATs do not predict school performance very well even for Whites.
3.	B	309	Predictive validity refers to the extent to which standardized tests accurately predict later college grades.
4.	A	310	Herrnstein and Murray, in *The Bell Curve*, argue that intelligence is inherited.
5.	D	311	The process, which is commonly found in U.S. schools, of separating students on the basis of their performance on some measure of cognitive ability is tracking or ability grouping.
6.	C	312	The effect of teacher expectations on a student's performance, independent of the student's actual ability, is the labeling effect.
7.	A	312	The effect of teacher expectations on a student's actual performance, independent of the student's actual ability, is the teacher expectancy effect.
8.	B	314	Teachers tend to treat Black women and White women differently.
9.	A	314	The economy of a society is the system by which goods and services are produced, distributed, and consumed.
10.	C	315	Service industry is a broad term, meant to encompass a wide range of economic activities now common in the labor market, including banking and finance, retail sales, hotel and restaurant work, and healthcare.
11.	D	315	An economic system based on the principles of market competition, private property, and the pursuit of profit is capitalism.
12.	B	316	In pure communism, industry is not the private property of owners. Rather, the state is the sole owner of the systems of production.
13.	A	316	The concept of the global economy acknowledges that all dimensions of the economy now cross national borders, including investment, production, management, markets, labor, information, and technology.
14.	B	316	The fear and hatred of foreigners is xenophobia.
15.	D	316	The term economic restructuring refers to the contemporary transformations in the basic structure of work that are permanently altering the workplace.

16.	C	317	The term deindustrialization refers to the transition from a predominantly goods-producing economy to one based on the provision of services.
17.	D	318	The process by which human labor is replaced by machines is known as automation, eliminates many repetitive and tiresome tasks, and makes rapid communication and access to information possible.
18.	A	318	A side effect of automation and technological progress in which the level of skill required to perform certain jobs declines over time is deskilling.
19.	B	318	Sociologists define work as productive human activity that creates something of value, either goods or services.
20.	C	319	Work that is specifically intended to produce a desired state of mind in a client is
21.	A	321	Conflict theorists view the transformations that are taking place in the workplace as the result of inherent tensions in the social systems, tensions that arise from the power differences between groups vying for social and economic resources.
22.	B	321	The feeling of powerlessness and separation from society is alienation.
23.	D	322	One of the most dramatic changes in the labor force since World War II has been the number of women employed. The percentage of employed Black and White women has converged in recent years, so that both are now equally likely to be employed. The Family and Medical Leave Act of 1993 has forced companies to write more progressive policies for family and medical leaves for their employees, although studies show that few workers are able to take advantage of this policy, because they cannot afford the time without pay.
24.	B	323	The percentage of those people who are not working but are officially defined as looking for work comprise the unemployment rate.
25.	C	325	Dual labor market theory views the labor market as comprising two major segments: the primary labor market and the secondary labor market.
26.	A	326	Many service jobs, such as waiting tables, nonunionized assembly work, and domestic work, are in the secondary labor market.
27.	A	327	The glass ceiling refers to the invisible barriers which prevent women and minorities from substantial advancement in corporate bureaucracies.
28.	D	327	Sexual harassment is defined as unwanted physical or verbal sexual behavior that occurs in the context of a relationship of unequal power and that is experienced as a threat to the victim's job or educational activities.
29.	D	330	The Americans with Disabilities Act of 1973 protects disabled people from discrimination in employment and stipulates that employers and other providers, such as schools and public transportation systems, must provide "reasonable accommodation" for disabled persons. The law prohibits employers with fifteen or more employees from discriminating against either job applicants who are disabled or current employees who become disabled. Disabled people report that they are often ignored and treated as if they are invisible in the workplace.
30.	B	326	Occupational prestige is the perceived social value of an occupation in the eyes of the general public.

ANSWERS TO THE TRUE-FALSE STATEMENTS.

1.	F	304	Compulsory education is a relatively new idea. During the nineteenth century, many states did not yet have laws requiring education for everyone.
2.	T	307	In the general population, there is a strong correlation between formal education and occupation, although the relationship is not perfect.
3.	T	308	In the U.S., students from lower-class families have lower average scores on exams such as the Scholastic Assessment Test (SAT).
4.	F	310	In general, Whites tend to score higher on IQ tests and SATs than minorities, men score higher than women, and the higher a person's social class, the higher the test score.
5.	T	311	The detracking movement is based on the eblief that including students of varying

			cognitive abilities is more beneficial to students than tracking, especially for students in junior high and high schools.
6.	T	313	When teachers have high expectations for students, they call on them more, praise them more often, and interact with them more frequently.
7.	T	315	While industrialized societies are primarily organized around the production of goods, postindustrialized societies are organized around the provision of services.
8.	F	315	Within capitalist societies, stockholders own corporations or a share of the corporations' wealth.
9.	F	316	With the new international division of labor, research and development are primarily done in the U.S., Japan, Germany, and other major world powers.
10.	F	316	Women and racial minorities are expected to comprise way over one-half of the labor force by the year 2005.
11.	T	317	In a labor market experiencing deindustrialization, there is job growth in professional and administrative positions with higher educational requirements and in some manufacturing jobs that require specific technological training.
12.	F	323	The group experiencing the greatest unemployment in the U.S. currently is Native Americans.
13.	T	328	Recent Supreme Court cases have upheld that same-sex harassment also falls under federal legislation, as does harassment directed by women against men.
14.	F	326	Jobs that employ mostly women are lower in prestige than those that employ more men.
15.	T	321	The labor performed by racial minority groups has often been the lowest paid, least prestigious, and most arduous work.

Chapter Thirteen

GOVERNMENT AND HEALTH CARE

Multiple-Choice Questions. Select the best response.

1. The _____ is an abstract concept that includes all those institutions that represent official power in society, such as the government and its legal system, the police, and the military.
    a. political system
    b. state
    c. federation
    d. constituency

2. _____ is a fundamental type of formal social control that outlines what is permissible and what is forbidden.
    a. Law
    b. The Golden Rule
    c. The criminal justice system
    d. Prison

3. Information which is disseminated by a group or organization which is intended to justify its own power is:
    a. advertising
    b. agenda
    c. propaganda
    d. illegal, unless it is factually accurate

4. _____ is power that is perceived by others as legitimate.
    a. Authority
    b. Government
    c. Influence
    d. Charisma

5. The ability of one person or a group to exercise influence and control over others is:
    a. authority
    b. charisma
    c. power
    d. control

6. Max Weber believed that _____ authority stems from long-established patterns that give certain people or groups legitimate power in society.
    a. charismatic
    b. traditional
    c. rational-legal
    d. legal-rational

7. A type of formal organization characterized by an authority hierarchy, a clear division of labor, explicit rules, and impersonality is a(n):
    a. corporation
    b. constituency
    c. aggregate
    d. bureaucracy

8.   The _____ model interprets power in society as derived from the representation of diverse interests of different groups in society.
   a. pluralist
   b. power elite
   c. autonomous state
   d. feminist

9.   Any constituency in society organized to promote its own agenda, including large, nationally based groups such as the National Organization for Women (NOW) is a(n):
   a. bureaucracy
   b. political action committee (PACs)
   c. interest group
   d. corporation

10.   Groups of people who organize to support candidates they feel will represent their views comprise:
   a. corporations
   b. political action committees (PACs)
   c. bureaucracies
   d. interest groups

11.   The power elite model, based on the work of Karl Marx, argues that the true power structure of a society consists of people well positioned in the:
   a. economy
   b. government
   c. military
   d. all of the above

12.   The _____ model interprets the state as its own major constituent, which develops its own interests. Further, the state seeks to promote its own interests, independent of other interests and the public that it allegedly serves.
   a. pluralist
   b. power elite
   c. autonomous state
   d. feminist

13.   _____ are organizational linkages created when the same people sit on the boards of directors of a number of different corporations.
   a. Interlocking directorates
   b. Interest groups
   c. Political action committees (PACs)
   d. Expressive groups

14.   The _____ includes those state institutions that represent the population, making rules that govern the society.
   a. federation
   b. municipality
   c. government
   d. nation

15.   A government that is based on the principle of representing all people through the right to vote is a:
   a. totalitarian state
   b. socialist state
   c. communist state
   d. democratic state

16. The term _____ refers to the differences in men's and women's political attitudes and behavior.
    a. gender disparity
    b. gender gap
    c. sexual separation
    d. gender divergence

17. The _____ program, begun in 1965 under the administration of Lyndon Johnson, provides medical insurance covering hospital costs for all individuals age sixty-five or older.
    a. Medicare
    b. Medicost
    c. Medicaid
    d. Hospicare

18. _____ is an eating disorder characterized by compulsive dieting.
    a. Bulimia
    b. Calista Flockhart Syndrome
    c. Anorexia
    d. Karen Carpenter Disease

19. The famous study, begun by the U.S. Health Service in 1932, which inadvertently revealed the relationship between race and the treatment of illness in our society, is the:
    a. Howard University Sickle Cell Study
    b. Tuskegee Syphilis Study
    c. National Cancer Diagnosis and Treatment Study
    d. Georgetown Epidemiology Survey

20. Which of the following statements about social class and health care is (are) TRUE?
    a. Part of the reasons for different rates of some illnesses in different social classes lies in personal habits. For example, those of higher socioeconomic status smoke more, and smoking is the major cause of lung cancer and an important contributor to cardiovascular disease.
    b. Poor living conditions, elevated levels of pollution in lower-income neighborhoods, stress caused by financial troubles, and a lack of access to healthcare facilities all contribute to the high rate of disease among the lower classes.
    c. The wealthy are more subject to psychological stress in general than the middle or lower classes.
    d. All of the above

21. _____ occurs when an individual is socially devalued because of some malady, illness, misfortune or similar attribute.
    a. Stereotyping
    b. Discrimination
    c. Prejudice
    d. Stigma

22. The term for a category of disorders that result from a breakdown of the body's immune system is:
    a. AIDS (acquired immune deficiency syndrome)
    b. AIDS (achieved immune deficit syndrome)
    c. HIV (human immune virus)
    d. syphilis

23. The movement which removed many psychiatric patients from hospitals in the 1960s and early 1970s and relocated them in smaller, community-based facilities, is the _____ movement.
    a. community care
    b. half-way house
    c. deinstitutionalization
    d. humanitarian care

24. The process by which society, following the medical profession, assigns all aspects of health and illness an exclusively medical meaning is:
   a. professionalization
   b. physician empowerment
   c. the most effective and efficient method to diagnose and treat symptoms
   d. medicalization

25. The pattern of expectations that society applies to one who is ill is the:
   a. patient role
   b. sick role
   c. sick status
   d. patient status

26. According to the _____ perspective on the sociology of health, government policies should improve access to healthcare for minority racial-ethnic groups, the poor, and women.
   a. conflict
   b. functionalist
   c. symbolic interaction
   d. labeling

27. Private clinical care organizations that provide medical services in exchange for a set membership fee, and thereby have direct responsibility and control over costs incurred, are:
   a. physician assistance programs
   b. health insurance organizations
   c. health maintenance organizations (HMOs)
   d. medical corporations

28. To protect themselves against potential malpractice suits, doctors increasingly practice _____ medicine, which entails ordering excessively thorough tests, X rays, etc. at the least indication that something may be wrong, partly to insure that nothing is missed and partly to document that the highest possible level of care was given.
   a. protective
   b. defensive
   c. liability-aware
   d. proactive

29. Under _____, a plan recommended by the Clinton administration, all individuals in the U.S. would belong to a complex of managed-care organizations, rather like HMOs, that would use their collective bargaining force to drive down the cost of health insurance, while accepting responsibility for operating their own facilities in an economical manner and continuing to provide high-quality care.
   a. managed competition
   b. federal competition
   c. medical competition
   d. socialist medicine

30. The act of killing a severely ill person as an act of mercy is:
   a. homicide
   b. infanticide
   c. euthanasia
   d. legal in six states in the U.S.

True-False Statements.

1. The movement to censor sexually explicit materials on the Internet is an example of state-based censorship.

2. Authority is the ability of one person or group to exercise influence and control over others.

3. Rational-legal leaders are often believed to have special gifts, even magical powers, and their presumed personal attributes inspire devotion and obedience.

4. The pluralist model of power, based on the work of C. Wright Mills, argues that the power structure consists of people well-positioned in the economy, the government, and the military.

5. Some feminist theorists see the state as fundamentally patriarchal and argue that its organization embodies the fixed principle that men are more powerful than women.

6. In general, the lower a person's socioeconomic status in the U.S., the higher the likelihood that she or he will vote.

7. Many members of Congress are millionaires and most are well-educated White men, from upper-middle or upper income backgrounds, and have an Anglo-Saxon Protestant heritage.

8. The military arm of the state is among the most powerful and influential social institutions in almost all societies, including the United States.

9. The incorporation of women into the U.S. military has changed the look of the military, but it is still a highly masculine institution in terms of personnel and policies.

10. Medicare is a governmental program that provides medical care in the form of health insurance for the poor, those on welfare, and for the disabled.

11. The eating disorder characterized by alternate binge eating and then purging or induced vomiting to lose weight is anorexia.

12. Among women, African Americans are more likely than Whites to fall victim to diseases such as cancer, heart disease, stroke, and diabetes and have a three times greater rate of maternal mortality during childbirth than Whites.

13. Based on National Opinion Research Center data, nearly 12% of American adult males report sex with a prostitute in the last year.

14. A rising number of patients are suing their physicians in the U.S. In response, physicians are increasing their malpractice insurance to protect themselves.

15. Positive or "active" euthanasia involves withholding medical treatment with the knowledge that doing so will produce the death of the patient.

Short-Answer Questions.
A page reference to the relevant text material is provided in the parenthesis.

1. List, describe, and provide one example of a leader who represents each of the three types of authority in society postulated by Max Weber (336).

2. Compare and contrast the following theories of power: pluralist model, power elite model, autonomous state model, and feminist theories of the state (338).

96

3. Discuss the role of the military in the state. As a social institution, how do race, gender, and sexual orientation affect the military in the U.S. (344)?

4. Discuss the relationship between health care and race, social class, and gender. What policies would you recommend to reduce these disparities (350)?

5. List and discuss the three prominent problems with the U.S. healthcare system identified by functionalist theorists and presented in the textbook (356).

ANSWERS TO THE MULTIPLE-CHOICE QUESTIONS.

1. B 334 The state is an abstract concept that includes all those institutions that represent official power in society, such as the government and its legal system, the police, and the military.
2. A 335 Law is a fundamental type of formal social control that outlines what is permissible and what is forbidden.
3. C 335 Information which is disseminated by a group or organization which is intended to justify its own power is propaganda.
4. A 335 Authority is power that is perceived by others as legitimate.
5. C 335 The ability of one person or a group to exercise influence and control over others is power.
6. B 336 Max Weber believed that traditional authority stems from long-established patterns that give certain people or groups legitimate power in society.
7. D 336 A type of formal organization characterized by an authority hierarchy, a clear division of labor, explicit rules, and impersonality is a bureaucracy.
8. A 338 The pluralist model interprets power in society as derived from the representation of diverse interests of different groups in society.
9. C 338 Any constituency in society organized to promote its own agenda, including large, nationally based groups such as the National Organization for Women (NOW) is an interest group.
10. B 339 Groups of people who organize to support candidates they feel will represent their views comprise political action committees (PACs).
11. D 339 The power elite model, based on the work of Karl Marx, argues that the true power structure of a society consists of people well positioned in the economy, government, and the military.
12. C 339 The autonomous state model interprets the state as its own major constituent, which develops its own interests. Further, the state seeks to promote its own interests, independent of other interests and the public that it allegedly serves.
13. A 339 Interlocking directorates are organizational linkages created when the same people sit on the boards of directors of a number of different corporations.
14. C 340 The government includes those state institutions that represent the population, making rules that govern the society.
15. D 340 A government that is based on the principle of representing all people through the right to vote is a democratic state.
16. B 342 The term gender gap refers to the differences in men's and women's political attitudes and behavior.
17. A 349 The Medicare program, begun in 1965 under the administration of Lyndon Johnson, provides medical insurance covering hospital costs for all individuals age sixty-five or older.
18. C 349 Anorexia is an eating disorder characterized by compulsive dieting.
19. B 350 The famous study, begun by the U.S. Health Service in 1932, which inadvertently revealed the relationship between race and the treatment of illness in our society, is the Tuskegee Syphilis Study.
20. B 351 Poor living conditions, elevated levels of pollution in lower-income neighborhoods,

stress caused by financial troubles, and a lack of access to healthcare facilities all contribute to the high rate of disease among the lower classes.

21.	D	353	Stigma occurs when an individual is socially devalued because of some malady, illness, misfortune or similar attribute.
22.	A	354	The term for a category of disorders that result from a breakdown of the body's immune system is AIDS (acquired immune deficiency syndrome).
23.	C	355	The movement which removed many psychiatric patients from hospitals in the 1960s and early 1970s and relocated them in smaller, community-based facilities, is the deinstitutionalization movement.
24.	D	355	The process by which society, following the medical profession, assigns all aspects of health and illness an exclusively medical meaning is medicalization.
25.	B	356	The pattern of expectations that society applies to one who is ill is the sick role.
26.	A	356	According to the conflict perspective on the sociology of health, government policies should improve access to healthcare for minority racial-ethnic groups, the poor, and women.
27.	C	358	Private clinical care organizations that provide medical services in exchange for a set membership fee, and thereby have direct responsibility and control over costs incurred, are health maintenance organizations (HMOs).
28.	B	359	To protect themselves against potential malpractice suits, doctors increasingly practice defensive medicine, which entails ordering excessively thorough tests, X rays, etc. at the least indication that something may be wrong, partly to insure that nothing is missed and partly to document that the highest possible level of care was given.
29.	A	360	Under managed competition, a plan recommended by the Clinton administration, all individuals in the U.S. would belong to a complex of managed-care organizations, rather like HMOs, that would use their collective bargaining force to drive down the cost of health insurance, while accepting responsibility for operating their own facilities in an economical manner and continuing to provide high-quality care.
30.	C	361	The act of killing a severely ill person as an act of mercy is euthanasia.

ANSWERS TO THE TRUE-FALSE STATEMENTS.

1.	T	335	The movement to censor sexually explicit materials on the Internet is an example of state-based censorship.
2.	F	335	Power is the ability of one person or group to exercise influence and control over others.
3.	F	336	Charismatic leaders are often believed to have special gifts, even magical powers, and their presumed personal attributes inspire devotion and obedience.
4.	F	339	The power elite model of power, based on the work of C. Wright Mills, argues that the power structure consists of people well-positioned in the economy, the government, and the military.
5.	T	340	Some feminist theorists see the state as fundamentally patriarchal and argue that its organization embodies the fixed principle that men are more powerful than women.
6.	F	340	In general, the higher a person's socioeconomic status in the U.S., the higher the likelihood that she or he will vote.
7.	T	342	Many members of Congress are millionaires and most are well-educated White men, from upper-middle or upper income backgrounds, and have an Anglo-Saxon Protestant heritage.
8.	T	344	The military arm of the state is among the most powerful and influential social institutions in almost all societies, including the United States.
9.	T	346	The incorporation of women into the U.S. military has changed the look of the military, but it is still a highly masculine institution in terms of personnel and policies.
10.	F	348	Medicaid is a governmental program that provides medical care in the form of health insurance for the poor, those on welfare, and for the disabled.
11.	F	348	The eating disorder characterized by alternate binge eating and then purging or induced vomiting to lose weight is bulimia.

12.	T	350	Among women, African Americans are more likely than Whites to fall victim to diseases such as cancer, heart disease, stroke, and diabetes and have a three times greater rate of maternal mortality during childbirth than Whites.
13.	F	352	Based on National Opinion Research Center data, only 0.6% of American adult males report sex with a prostitute in the last year.
14.	T	359	A rising number of patients are suing their physicians in the U.S. In response, physicians are increasing their malpractice insurance to protect themselves.
15.	F	361	Negative or "passive" euthanasia involves withholding medical treatment with the knowledge that doing so will produce the death of the patient.

Chapter Fourteen

RELIGION

Multiple-Choice Questions. Select the best response.

1.   According to sociologists, an institutional system of symbols, beliefs, values, and practices by which a group of people interprets and responds to what they feel is sacred and that provides answers to questions of ultimate meaning is:
   a.   a cult
   b.   an ideology
   c.   religion
   d.   a sect

2.   A _____ is an object or living thing that a religious group regards with special awe and reverence.
   a.   totem
   b.   ritual
   c.   medal
   d.   crucifix

3.   Which of the following statements about religion is (are) TRUE?
   a.   Religion establishes values and moral proscriptions for behavior.
   b.   Religion provides answers to questions of ultimate meaning.
   c.   Religion is an institutional feature of groups.
   d.   All of the above

4.   _____ beliefs, the ordinary beliefs of daily life, may be institutionalized, but they are specifically not religious.
   a.   Secular
   b.   Monotheistic
   c.   Sacred
   d.   Charismatic

5.   The intensity and consistency of the practicing of a person's or group's faith is:
   a.   their religious commitment
   b.   religiosity
   c.   ideology
   d.   polytheism

6.   The worship of more than one deity is:
   a.   bitheism
   b.   monotheism
   c.   polytheism
   d.   multitheism

7.   Those religions in which beliefs and practices are based on male power and authority are:
   a.   patritheistic
   b.   patriarchal
   c.   matriarchal
   d.   matritheistic

8. Emile Durkheim argued that religion is _____ for society because it reaffirms the social bonds that people have with each other, which creates social cohesion and social integration.
    a.   important
    b.   necessary
    c.   beneficial
    d.   functional

9. Religious _____ are symbolic activities that express a group's spiritual convictions.
    a.   rituals
    b.   totems
    c.   ceremonies
    d.   pilgrimages

10. The body of beliefs that are common to a community or society and that give people a sense of belonging comprise what Durkheim referred to as their:
    a.   belief system
    b.   ideology
    c.   collective consciousness
    d.   religiosity

11. According to Max Weber, the religious belief that relentless work was a means of confirming and demonstrating one's salvation is the:
    a.   Protestant Ethic
    b.   American Dream
    c.   Capitalist Conception
    d.   Foundation of Catholicism

12. Religious _____ is the excessive belief in the superiority of one's religious group.
    a.   charisma
    b.   ideology
    c.   discrimination
    d.   ethnocentrism

13. To Marx, religion is a(n) _____, or a belief system that legitimates the social order and supports the ideas of the ruling class.
    a.   sacred philosophy
    b.   ideology
    c.   theology
    d.   divine revelation

14. According to the _____ theory, religion is socially constructed and emerges with historical and social change.
    a.   symbolic interaction
    b.   conflict
    c.   functionalist
    d.   religious socialization

15. If measured in terms of numbers of followers, the largest religion in the world is:
    a.   Buddhism
    b.   Judaism
    c.   Christianity
    d.   Hinduism

16.   The principal categories of Protestantism include:
    a.   fundamentalists
    b.   Catholics
    c.   Jews
    d.   all of the above

17.   An example of the transformation of the Catholic Church is the emergence of _____, which is an inspiration of Catholic priests in Latin America who feel that the Gospel of Christ commands the church to lead in liberating the poor and the oppressed of the world.
    a.   Marxist theology
    b.   liberation theology
    c.   radical theology
    d.   revolution theology

18.   Followers of the _____ religion are called Muslims.
    a.   Catholic
    b.   Buddhist
    c.   Hindu
    d.   Islamic

19.   According to _____ principles, those who live the most ideal life are seen as part of the higher caste, with the lower caste of "untouchables" being viewed as spiritually bereft.
    a.   Catholic
    b.   Buddhist
    c.   Hindu
    d.   Islamic

20.   Which of the following statements about religious identification is (are) TRUE?
    a.   Older people are more likely than younger people to express no religious preference.
    b.   Those in higher income brackets are more likely to identify as Catholics or Jews than those in lower-income brackets, who are more likely to identify as Protestant, although these trends vary among Protestants by denomination.
    c.   Fundamentalist Protestants are more likely to come from higher income groups than Protestants in general.
    d.   All of the above

21.   _____ are formal organizations that tend to see themselves, and are seen by society, as the primary and legitimate religious institutions.
    a.   Churches
    b.   Sects
    c.   Cults
    d.   Ideologies

22.   Religious groups that typically develop in protest against events or beliefs within the secular world are:
    a.   churches
    b.   sects
    c.   cults
    d.   ideologies

23.   The quality attributed to individuals believed by their followers to have special powers is:
    a.   charisma
    b.   personality
    c.   magic
    d.   magnetism

24. The process by which one learns a particular faith is:
    a. brainwashing
    b. religious education
    c. indoctrination
    d. religious socialization

25. _____ is a transformation of religious identity, which can be a private or public process, subtle or dramatic.
    a. Brainwashing
    b. Religious socialization
    c. Conversion
    d. Polytheism

26. The _____ claims that innocent people are tricked into religious conversion and that religious cults manipulate and coerce people into accepting their beliefs.
    a. irrational behavior theory
    b. brainwashing thesis
    c. mind control syndrome
    d. psychologically vulnerable theory

27. _____ emphasizes that conversion is linked to shifting patterns of association, not simply mind control. People are active participants in the process of their own conversion.
    a. Religious socialization
    b. The brainwashing thesis
    c. Charismatic transformation theory
    d. Social drift theory

28. A(n) _____, characteristic of many Quakers, Unitarians, and Jews, features a searching attitude toward religion.
    a. quest orientation
    b. agnostic philosophy
    c. weak religious commitment
    d. seeking approach

29. The fear and hatred of homosexuals, known as _____, has been linked to religious belief.
    a. sexual orientation insecurity
    b. transsexuality
    c. homophobia
    d. gender ambiguity

30. _____ is the belief or behavior that defines Jewish people as inferior and targets them for stereotypes, mistreatment, and acts of hatred.
    a. Anti-miscegenation
    b. Anti-Semitism
    c. Judaphobia
    d. Discrimination

True-False Statements.

1. Despite the U.S. Constitution's principle of the separation of church and state, Christian religious beliefs and practices dominate American culture.

2. Seventy percent of Americans say they are a member of a church or synagogue, although only 43 percent say they attend a church or synagogue weekly or almost weekly.

3. Christianity is a patriarchal religion; the ascendancy of man is emphasized in the role of women in the church, the instruction given on relations between the sexes, and even the language of worship itself.

4. Marx believed that religion binds individuals to their society by establishing a collective consciousness.

5. Emile Durkheim identified the role of the Protestant Ethic and its emphasis on the value of hard work in the development of capitalism.

6. Principles of Christianity legitimated the system of slavery in the eyes of the slaveowners by arguing that slaves were being rescued from damnation and exposed to the Christian way of life.

7. Recently, mainline Protestants in the United States have seen increases in church membership and attendance.

8. There are significant divisions of culture and practice within Judaism, since Conservative Jews, a small fraction of the total number of U.S. Jews, adhere strictly to a traditional conception of their religious faith and Orthodox Jews have a more secular orientation.

9. In general, the most likely persons to be unaffiliated with any church are young, White, well-educated, non-Southern men who move frequently.

10. The Branch Davidians, led by David Koresh, were a good example of as sect.

11. One of the strongest influences on religious socialization is the family. Even when religious beliefs are not explicitly taught through family-based rituals, children learn the beliefs of their parents.

12. In the first phase of a religious conversion, the potential convert typically has an experience when she or he perceives as disruptive to their previous life, which allows them to be open to a serious change in their social environment.

13. An intrinsic religious orientation denotes an exclusionary and highly devout religious attitude, such as that of fundamentalist religious groups.

14. Protestants are more likely than Catholics to think that a homosexual relationship between consenting adults is an acceptable lifestyle and should be legal.

15. Like other forms of prejudice, anti-Semitism is associated with a characteristic social-psychological profile, which includes authoritarianism, aggression, generalized hostility, having conventional values, and having a preoccupation with dominance and submission.

Short-Answer Questions.
A page reference to the relevant text material is provided in the parenthesis.

1. Define religion. List and discuss the six characteristics of religion presented in the textbook (365).

2. Compare and contrast the following theories of religion: Emile Durkheim, Max Weber, and Karl Marx. Include in your discussion Durkheim's perspectives on rituals and the collective consciousness, Weber's concept of the Protestant Ethic, and Marx's analysis of religion as an ideology (370).

3. Define and provide one example of each of the following religious organizations: churches, sects, and cults (378).

4. Define and describe the process of religious socialization. Distinguish between informal religious socialization and formal religious socialization (380).

104

5.   Define religious conversion. Compare and contrast the brainwashing thesis and the social drift theory of conversion. Summarize the phases of religious conversion, according to social drift theorists, and the phases of deconversion (381).

ANSWERS TO THE MULTIPLE-CHOICE QUESTIONS.

1.	C	365	According to sociologists, an institutional system of symbols, beliefs, values, and practices by which a group of people interprets and responds to what they feel is sacred and that provides answers to questions of ultimate meaning is religion.
2.	A	366	A totem is an object or living thing that a religious group regards with special awe and reverence.
3.	D	365	Religion provides answers to questions of ultimate meaning. Religion establishes values and moral proscriptions for behavior. Religion is an institutional feature of groups.
4.	A	366	Secular beliefs, the ordinary beliefs of daily life, may be institutionalized, but they are specifically not religious.
5.	B	368	The intensity and consistency of the practicing of a person's or group's faith is religiosity.
6.	C	369	The worship of more than one deity is polytheism.
7.	B	369	Those religions in which beliefs and practices are based on male power and authority are patriarchal.
8.	D	370	Emile Durkheim argued that religion is functional for society because it reaffirms the social bonds that people have with each other, which creates social cohesion and social integration.
9.	A	370	Religious rituals are symbolic activities that express a group's spiritual convictions.
10.	C	370	The body of beliefs that are common to a community or society and that give people a sense of belonging comprise what Durkheim referred to as their collective consciousness.
11.	A	371	According to Max Weber, the religious belief that relentless work was a means of confirming and demonstrating one's salvation is the Protestant Ethic.
12.	D	371	Religious ethnocentrism is the excessive belief in the superiority of one's religious group.
13.	B	372	To Marx, religion is an ideology, or a belief system that legitimates the social order and supports the ideas of the ruling class.
14.	A	372	According to the symbolic interaction theory, religion is socially constructed and emerges with historical and social change.
15.	C	372	If measured in terms of numbers of followers, the largest religion in the world is Christianity.
16.	A	374	The principal categories of Protestantism include fundamentalists.
17.	B	375	An example of the transformation of the Catholic Church is the emergence of liberation theology, which is an inspiration of Catholic priests in Latin America who feel that the Gospel of Christ commands the church to lead in liberating the poor and the oppressed of the world.
18.	D	376	Followers of the Islamic religion are called Muslims.
19	C	376.	According to Hindu principles, those who live the most ideal life are seen as part of the higher caste, with the lower caste of "untouchables" being viewed as spiritually bereft.
20.	B	377	Those in higher income brackets are more likely to identify as Catholics or Jews than those in lower-income brackets, who are more likely to identify as Protestant, although these trends vary among Protestants by denomination.
21.	A	378	Churches are formal organizations that tend to see themselves, and are seen by society, as the primary and legitimate religious institutions.
22.	B	378	Religious groups that typically develop in protest against events or beliefs within the secular world are sects.
23.	A	379	The quality attributed to individuals believed by their followers to have special powers is charisma.
24.	D	379	The process by which one learns a particular faith is religious socialization.
25.	C	381	Conversion is a transformation of religious identity, which can be a private or public process, subtle or dramatic.
26.	B	382	The brainwashing thesis claims that innocent people are tricked into religious conversion

			and that religious cults manipulate and coerce people into accepting their beliefs.
27.	D	382	Social drift theory emphasizes that conversion is linked to shifting patterns of association, not simply mind control. People are active participants in the process of their own conversion.
28	A	383.	A quest orientation, characteristic of many Quakers, Unitarians, and Jews, features a searching attitude toward religion.
29.	C	384	The fear and hatred of homosexuals, known as homophobia, has been linked to religious belief.
30.	B	384	Anti-Semitism is the belief or behavior that defines Jewish people as inferior and targets them for stereotypes, mistreatment, and acts of hatred.

ANSWERS TO THE TRUE-FALSE STATEMENTS.

1.	T	367	Despite the U.S. Constitution's principle of the separation of church and state, Christian religious beliefs and practices dominate American culture.
2.	T	368	Seventy percent of Americans say they are a member of a church or synagogue, although only 43 percent say they attend a church or synagogue weekly or almost weekly.
3.	T	369	Christianity is a patriarchal religion; the ascendancy of man is emphasized in the role of women in the church, the instruction given on relations between the sexes, and even the language of worship itself.
4.	F	370	Durkheim believed that religion binds individuals to their society by establishing a collective consciousness.
5.	F	371	Max Weber identified the role of the Protestant Ethic and its emphasis on the value of hard work in the development of capitalism.
6.	T	372	Principles of Christianity legitimated the system of slavery in the eyes of the slaveowners by arguing that slaves were being rescued from damnation and exposed to the Christian way of life.
7.	F	374	Recently, mainline Protestants in the United States have seen declines in church membership and attendance.
8.	F	375	There are significant divisions of culture and practice within Judaism, since Orthodox Jews, a small fraction of the total number of U.S. Jews, adhere strictly to a traditional conception of their religious faith and Reform Jews have a more secular orientation.
9.	T	377	In general, the most likely persons to be unaffiliated with any church are young, White, well-educated, non-Southern men who move frequently.
10.	F	379	The Branch Davidians, led by David Koresh, were a good example of as cult.
11.	T	380	One of the strongest influences on religious socialization is the family. Even when religious beliefs are not explicitly taught through family-based rituals, children learn the beliefs of their parents.
12.	T	381	In the first phase of a religious conversion, the potential convert typically has an experience when she or he perceives as disruptive to their previous life, which allows them to be open to a serious change in their social environment.
13.	F	383	An extrinsic religious orientation denotes an exclusionary and highly devout religious attitude, such as that of fundamentalist religious groups.
14.	T	384	Protestants are more likely than Catholics to think that a homosexual relationship between consenting adults is an acceptable lifestyle and should be legal.
15.	T	384	Like other forms of prejudice, anti-Semitism is associated with a characteristic social-psychological profile, which includes authoritarianism, aggression, generalized hostility, having conventional values, and having a preoccupation with dominance and submission.

Chapter Fifteen

POPULATION, URBANISM, AND THE ENVIRONMENT

1. The scientific study of population is:
    a. ecology
    b. sociology
    c. demography
    d. numerology

2. A head count of the entire population of a country, usually done at regular intervals is a(n):
    a. census
    b. cohort
    c. centennial
    d. aggregate

3. _____ include information about births, marriages, deaths, migrations in and out of the country, and other fundamental questions related to population.
    a. Census data
    b. Official statistics
    c. Government statistics
    d. Vital statistics

4. Migration into a society from outside is:
    a. population shift
    b. immigration
    c. international migration
    d. emigration

5. The _____ of a population is the number of babies born each year for every 1000 members of the population or the number of births divided by the population, times 1000.
    a. crude birthrate
    b. birth coefficient
    c. actual birthrate
    d. fertility rate

6. The potential number of children in a population that could be born if every woman reproduced at her maximum biological capacity during the childbearing years is:
    a. fertility
    b. productive capacity
    c. always somewhat lower than the society's fecundity
    d. fecundity

7. The infant mortality rate:
    a. is the number of deaths per years of infants less than 1 year old for every 1000 live births.
    b. is a measure that tends to reflect the standard of living of a population.
    c. varies substantially, since the overall infant mortality rate in the U.S. is approximately 7 infant deaths for every 1000 live births and the rate in many developing countries, such as Kenya, can rise higher than 35 deaths per 1000 live births.
    d. all of the above

8. The _____ of a population or group is defined as the average number of years that the group can expect to live.
   a. anticipated longevity
   b. longevity expectation
   c. life expectancy
   d. a and b

9. Factors that affect the composition of a population include its:
   a. sex ratio
   b. age-sex pyramid
   c. gender ratio
   d. all of the above

10. The number of males per 100 females in a population is:
    a. the sex ratio
    b. the sex coefficient
    c. the proportion of males to females index
    d. affected by the higher infant mortality rate of girls

11. The age composition of the U.S. is undergoing significant changes, as more people are entering the 65-and-over age bracket, in a trend known as the:
    a. aging of America
    b. maturing of America
    c. graying of America
    d. debilitating of America

12. A graphic representation of the age and gender structure of a society is the:
    a. age-sex graph
    b. age-sex pyramid
    c. age-sex table
    d. age-sex index

13. A(n) _____ consists of all the persons born within a given period.
    a. birth cluster
    b. generation
    c. cohort
    d. age bracket

14. The belief that a population tends to grow faster than the subsistence needed to sustain it is a fundamental argument of _____ theory.
    a. Malthusian
    b. ecological density
    c. demographic transition
    d. human ecosystem

15. _____ theory proposes that countries pass through a consistent sequence of population patterns linked to the degree of development in the society, and ending with a situation in which the birthrates and death rates are both relatively low.
    a. Human ecosystem
    b. Malthusian
    c. Demographic shift
    d. Demographic transition

16. According to _____, author of *The Population Bomb*, worldwide population growth has outgrown food production and massive starvation is inevitable.
    a. Max Weber
    b. Karl Marx
    c. Paul Ehrlich
    d. Thomas Malthus

17. A state in which the combined birthrate and death rate of a population simply sustains the population at a steady level is:
    a. Stage 2 in demographic transition theory
    b. the population replacement level
    c. Stage 1 in demographic transition theory
    d. commonly found in African and Latin American societies

18. The theoretical perspective of demography and population growth which is the most optimistic about the future is:
    a. Malthusian
    b. Demographic Transition
    c. Human Ecosystem
    d. Zero Population Growth (ZPG)

19. Which of the following statements about family planning and population policy is (are) TRUE?
    a. As countries in general become more economically developed, their birthrates and average family size generally drop, as predicted by demographic transition theory.
    b. Countries in Stage 2, such as Bangladesh, which had a declining death rate because of rapid economic and medical developments but retained a high birthrate, have lately become very receptive to birth control programs.
    c. There is some cultural resistance from some U.S. racial and ethnic groups to government-sponsored contraceptive programs. These groups sometimes argue that contraceptive measures are genocidal and threaten the survival of group membership.
    d. All of the above

20. According to Herbert Gans, urban dwellers include _____, who are typically students, artists, writers, and musicians, who form a tightly knit community and who choose urban living to be near the city's cultural facilities.
    a. cosmopolites
    b. ethnic villagers
    c. the cultural elite
    d. the artistic community

21. _____ is the number of people per unit of area, usually per square mile.
    a. Population concentration
    b. Inhabitant mass
    b. Population density
    c. Resident concentration

22. The scientific study of the interdependencies that exist between humans and our physical environment is:
    a. human ecology
    b. demography
    c. ecological demography
    d. socio-ecology

23. Any system of interdependent parts that involves human beings in interaction with one another and the physical environment is a:
    a. society
    b. social system
    c. human ecosystem
    d. social ecosystem

24. Which of the following statements about environmental pollution is (are) TRUE?
    a. The leading air polluters are the United States, Japan, Russia, and Poland.
    b. A huge portion of the pollutants released into the air come from the exhaust pipes of motor vehicles, which contains carbon monoxide, a highly toxic substance.
    c. The most threatening forms of pollution are the poisoning of the planet's air and water.
    d. All of the above

25. A rise in the earth's surface temperature caused by heat trapped by excess carbon dioxide in the atmosphere is known as:
    a. thermal pollution
    b. the greenhouse effect
    c. the hothouse contamination effect
    d. thermal waste

26. The heating of the earth's rivers and lakes as a result of the chemical discharges of heavy industry is:
    a. the greenhouse effect
    b. the industrial-waste effect
    c. thermal pollution
    d. industrial pollution

27. The scientific field of _____ combines the study of demography and ecology.
    a. ecological demography
    b. demographic ecology
    c. social demography
    d. social ecology

28. The departure of people from a society, which subtracts from the population, is:
    a. immigration
    b. migration
    c. external migration
    d. emigration

29. Which of the following statements about birthrates is (are) TRUE?
    a. In general, minority groups tend to have somewhat lower birthrates than White nonminority groups.
    b. Lower socioeconomic groups tend to have lower birthrates than those higher on the socioeconomic scale.
    c. Religious and cultural differences can affect birthrates. For example, Catholics have a higher birthrate than non-Catholics of the same socioeconomic status.
    d. All of the above

30. Which of the following statements about life expectancies and infant mortality is (are) TRUE?
    a. Men, on average, live longer than women.
    b. Inadequate health acre and health care facilities cause higher infant mortality rates and consequently the greater infant mortality among minorities and those in lower socioeconomic strata in the U.S. suggests that lack of adequate health care and adequate access to health facilities is one cause of the high infant mortality rates.
    c. African Americans, Hispanics, and Native Americans have a longer life expectancy than Whites.
    d. All of the above.

110

True-False Statements.

1. The total number of people in a society is determined by three variables: births, deaths, and migrations.

2. Because minorities tend to have higher birthrates in the U.S., assuming that present migration rates continue, and assuming that death rates do not outstrip birthrates, then the U.S. will have a significantly greater proportion of minorities, and thus a relatively lower proportion of Whites, in the future.

3. The recent patterns of migration for African Americans has been to the South and major Northern urban centers from the West, the Southwest, and New England.

4. In almost all societies, there are more boys born than girls, but because males have a higher death rate after infancy, there are usually more females than males in the overall population.

5. Countries with a high birthrate tend to have a high proportion of women in their childbearing years.

6. Malthus noted that populations tend to increase arithmetically, that is, by adding the same number of new individuals each year.

7. Malthusian theory predicted rather well the population changes of many agrarian societies such as Egypt from about AD 500 through the late 1700s.

8. According to demographic transition theorists, Stage 1 is characterized by a high birthrate but a low death rate.

9. Due to the official opposition of the Catholic Church to contraception, the majority of U.S. Catholics do not practice forms of birth control forbidden by their church.

10. Today's urban underclass would encompass what Herbert Gans labeled ethnic villagers.

11. The practice of redlining by banks, which renders it impossible for a person of color to get a mortgage loan for a specific property, intensifies racial segregation, especially in the suburbs.

12. Examining ecosystems, scientists have concluded that the supply of many natural resources is finite and if one element of an ecosystem is disturbed, the entire system is disturbed.

13. The heating of the earth's rivers and lakes as a result of the chemical discharges of heavy industry is the greenhouse effect.

14. U.S. communities with the greatest number of toxic dumps have the highest concentrations of non-White residents.

15. The EPA estimates that 13 percent of rural Americans may be drinking water contaminated by agricultural runoff and the improper disposal of toxic substances in landfills.

Short-Answer Questions.
A page reference to the relevant text material is provided in the parenthesis.

1. List, define, and discuss the three basic demographic processed that determine the total number of people in a population (393).

2. Define and discuss the following terms related to population characteristics: sex ratio, age-sex pyramid, and cohorts (396).

3.   Compare and contrast the three major theories of population: Mathusian, demographic transition, and zero population growth. Include both the "positive" checks on population growth and the "negative" checks on population growth recommended by each theory (398).

4.   List and discuss the stages of population change, according to demographic transition theorists (400).

5.   List and describe the three categories of urban residents identified by Herbert Gans (404).

ANSWERS TO THE MULTIPLE-CHOICE QUESTIONS.

1.	C	392	The scientific study of population is demography.
2.	A	392	A head count of the entire population of a country, usually done at regular intervals is a census.
3.	D	393	Vital statistics include information about births, marriages, deaths, migrations in and out of the country, and other fundamental questions related to population.
4.	B	393	Migration into a society from outside is immigration.
5.	A	393	The crude birthrate of a population is the number of babies born each year for every 1000 members of the population or the number of births divided by the population, times 1000.
6.	D	394	The potential number of children in a population that could be born if every woman reproduced at her maximum biological capacity during the childbearing years is fecundity.
7.	D	394	The infant mortality rate is the number of deaths per years of infants less than 1 year old for every 1000 live births, a measure that tends to reflect the standard of living of a population, and varies substantially, since the overall infant mortality rate in the U.S. is approximately 7 infant deaths for every 1000 live births and the rate in many developing countries, such as Kenya, can rise higher than 35 deaths per 1000 live births.
8.	C	394	The life expectancy of a population or group is defined as the average number of years that the group can expect to live.
9.	D	396	Factors that affect the composition of a population include its sex ratio, age-sex pyramid, and gender ratio.
10.	A	396	The number of males per 100 females in a population is the sex ratio.
11.	C	397	The age composition of the U.S. is undergoing significant changes, as more people are entering the 65-and-over age bracket, in a trend known as the graying of America.
12.	B	396	A graphic representation of the age and gender structure of a society is the age-sex pyramid.
13.	C	397	A cohort consists of all the persons born within a given period.
14.	A	399	The belief that a population tends to grow faster than the subsistence needed to sustain it is a fundamental argument of Malthusian theory.
15.	D	400	Demographic transition theory proposes that countries pass through a consistent sequence of population patterns linked to the degree of development in the society, and ending with a situation in which the birthrates and death rates are both relatively low.
16.	C	401	According to Paul Ehrlich, author of *The Population Bomb*, worldwide population growth has outgrown food production and massive starvation is inevitable.
17.	B	402	A state in which the combined birthrate and death rate of a population simply sustains the population at a steady level is the population replacement level.
18.	D	402	The theoretical perspective of demography and population growth which is the most optimistic about the future is Zero Population Growth (ZPG).
19.	D	403	As countries in general become more economically developed, their birthrates and average family size generally drop, as predicted by demographic transition theory. Countries in Stage 2, such as Bangladesh, which had a declining death rate because of rapid economic and medical developments but retained a high birthrate, have lately become very receptive to birth control programs. There is some cultural resistance from some U.S. racial and ethnic groups to government-sponsored contraceptive programs. These groups sometimes argue that contraceptive measures are genocidal and threaten the survival of group membership.
20.	A	404	According to Herbert Gans, urban dwellers include cosmopolites, who are typically

students, artists, writers, and musicians, who form a tightly knit community and who choose urban living to be near the city's cultural facilities.

21.	C	404	Population density is the number of people per unit of area, usually per square mile.
22.	A	405	The scientific study of the interdependencies that exist between humans and our physical environment is human ecology.
23.	C	405	Any system of interdependent parts that involves human beings in interaction with one another and the physical environment is a human ecosystem.
24.	D	406	The leading air polluters are the United States, Japan, Russia, and Poland. A huge portion of the pollutants released into the air come from the exhaust pipes of motor vehicles, which contains carbon monoxide, a highly toxic substance. The most threatening forms of pollution are the poisoning of the planet's air and water.
25.	B	408	A rise in the earth's surface temperature caused by heat trapped by excess carbon dioxide in the atmosphere is known as the greenhouse effect.
26.	C	409	The heating of the earth's rivers and lakes as a result of the chemical discharges of heavy industry is thermal pollution.
27.	A	411	The scientific field of ecological demography combines the study of demography and ecology.
28.	D	393	The departure of people from a society, which subtracts from the population, is emigration.
29.	C	394	Religious and cultural differences can affect birthrates. For example, Catholics have a higher birthrate than non-Catholics of the same socioeconomic status.
30.	B	395	Inadequate health acre and health care facilities cause higher infant mortality rates and consequently the greater infant mortality among minorities and those in lower socioeconomic strata in the U.S. suggests that lack of adequate health care and adequate access to health facilities is one cause of the high infant mortality rates.

ANSWERS TO THE TRUE-FALSE STATEMENTS.

1.	T	393	The total number of people in a society is determined by three variables: births, deaths, and migrations.
2.	T	394	Because minorities tend to have higher birthrates in the U.S., assuming that present migration rates continue, and assuming that death rates do not outstrip birthrates, then the U.S. will have a significantly greater proportion of minorities, and thus a relatively lower proportion of Whites, in the future.
3.	F	396	The recent patterns of migration for African Americans has been from the South and major Northern urban centers to the West, the Southwest, and New England.
4.	T	396	In almost all societies, there are more boys born than girls, but because males have a higher death rate after infancy, there are usually more females than males in the overall population.
5.	T	397	Countries with a high birthrate tend to have a high proportion of women in their childbearing years.
6.	F	399	Malthus noted that populations tend to experience an exponential increase, in which the number of individuals added each year grows, with the larger population generating an even larger number of births with each passing year.
7.	T	399	Malthusian theory predicted rather well the population changes of many agrarian societies such as Egypt from about AD 500 through the late 1700s.
8.	F	400	According to demographic transition theorists, Stage 2 is characterized by a high birthrate but a low death rate.
9.	F	404	Despite the official opposition of the Catholic Church to contraception, many U.S. Catholics practice forms of birth control forbidden by their church.
10.	F	404	Today's urban underclass would encompass what Herbert Gans labeled the trapped.
11.	T	404	The practice of redlining by banks, which renders it impossible for a person of color to get a mortgage loan for a specific property, intensifies racial segregation, especially in the suburbs.
12.	T	406	Examining ecosystems, scientists have concluded that the supply of many natural

resources is finite and if one element of an ecosystem is disturbed, the entire system is disturbed.

13.	F	409	The heating of the earth's rivers and lakes as a result of the chemical discharges of heavy industry is thermal pollution.
14.	T	409	U.S. communities with the greatest number of toxic dumps have the highest concentrations of non-White residents.
15.	F	409	The EPA estimates that 63 percent of rural Americans may be drinking water contaminated by agricultural runoff and the improper disposal of toxic substances in landfills.

Chapter Sixteen

SOCIAL CHANGE AND SOCIAL MOVEMENTS

Multiple-Choice Questions. Select the best response.

1. The alterations of social interactions, institutions, stratification systems, and elements of culture over time is:
    a. cultural transformation
    b. social change
    c. cultural development
    d. social progression

2. Gradual transformations that occur on a broad scale and affect many aspects of society are:
    a. macrochanges
    b. urban changes
    c. microchanges
    d. social adjustments

3. Which of the following statements about social change is (are) TRUE?
    a. Social change is uneven, since different parts of a society do not change at the same rate.
    b. Social change often creates conflict.
    c. The onset and consequences of social change are often unforeseen.
    d. All of the above

4. According to Durkheim, cohesion based on similarity among members in a society creates:
    a. contractual solidarity
    b. organic solidarity
    c. mechanical solidarity
    d. a and b

5. According to _____ theorists, societies move from structurally simple, homogeneous societies, such as foraging or pastoral societies, to structurally more complex, heterogeneous societies, such as agricultural, industrial, and postindustrial societies.
    a. cyclical
    b. functionalist
    c. modernization
    d. conflict

6. The theory that argues that structural, institutional, and cultural development of a society can follow many evolutionary paths simultaneously, with the different paths all emerging from the circumstances of the society in question is:
    a. dependency
    b. multidimensional
    c. unidimensional
    d. cyclical

7. _____ theories of social change invoke patterns of social structure and culture that are believed to reoccur at more or less regular intervals.
    a. Patterned
    b. Dependency
    c. World systems
    d. Cyclical

8. According to Sorokin and Caplow, societies which stress practical approaches to reality and include hedonistic and sensual components are in the third phase of development which is known as the:
   a. sensate
   b. ideational
   c. idealistic
   d. basic

9. The theory that states that global development is a worldwide process affecting nearly all societies that have been touched by technological change is:
   a. cyclical theory
   b. world systems theory
   c. modernization theory
   d. dependency theory

10. According to Wallerstein, _____ theory argues that all nations are members of a world wide system of unequal political and economic relationships, which benefits the developed and technologically advanced countries at the expense of the less technologically advanced and less developed countries.
    a. world systems
    b. dependency
    c. global interdependence
    d. cyclical

11. _____ theory maintains that highly industrialized nations tend to imprison developing nations in dependent relationships rather than spurring the higher mobility of developing countries with transfers of technology and business acumen.
    a. World systems
    b. Global interdependence
    c. Functionalist
    d. Dependency

12. The process of social and cultural change that is initiated by industrialization and followed by increased social differentiation and division of labor is:
    a. postindustrialization
    b. modernization
    c. the industrial revolution
    d. economic progress

13. According to Tonnies, a society characterized by a sense of fellowship, strong personal ties, sturdy primary group memberships, and personal loyalty among group members is a _____ society.
    a. pastoral
    b. gesellschaft
    c. gemeinschaft
    d. tribal

14. According to Dahrendorf and Berger, modernization has produced _____, in which industrialization and bureaucracies reach exceedingly high levels.
    a. a postindustrial society
    b. a mass society
    c. future shock
    d. social and personal pathology

15. A personality orientation in which the individual is guided by internal principles and morals and is relatively impervious to the superficialities of those around him or her is:
    a.   other-directed
    b.   inner-directed
    c.   tradition-directed
    d.   society-directed

16. _____ is the transmission of cultural elements from one society or cultural group to another.
    a.   Cultural diffusion
    b.   Cultural borrow
    c.   Cultural theft
    d.   Cultural larceny

17. Which of the following factors can influence social change?
    a.   demographic changes
    b.   war
    c.   technological innovations
    d.   all of the above

18. _____ occurs when normal conventions cease to guide proper behavior and people establish new patterns of interaction and social structure.
    a.   A social movement
    b.   Collective behavior
    c.   A social change
    d.   Social mobility

19. Communication between persons and communication between persons and computers is known as:
    a.   technospeak
    b.   internet interaction
    c.   cyberspace
    d.   web-speak

20. Collective behavior:
    a.   may emerge spontaneously in response to a unique situation
    b.   is innovative and sometimes revolutionary
    c.   may include crowds, riots, disasters, fads, fashions, and social movements
    d.   all of the above

21. _____ movements, such as the White supremacy movement and the large number of hate groups in the United States, are attempts to resist change toward greater racial equality.
    a.   Reactionary
    b.   Reform
    c.   Traditional
    d.   Radical

22. _____ movements focus on the development of new meaning within individual lives rather than pursuing social change.
    a.   Reactionary
    b.   Reform
    c.   Personal transformation
    d.   Transcendence

23. Social movements, such as the environmental movement, that gay and lesbian movement, the civil rights movement, the animal rights movement, and the religious right movement, are examples of
_____ movements.
a.   Social change
b.   Reform
c.   Reactionary
d.   Radical

24. Those movements that seek change through legal or other mainstream political means and typically work within existing institutions are _____ movements.
a.   radical
b.   reactionary
c.   extremist
d.   reform

25. Social movements do not typically develop out of thin air. Which of the following characteristics must typically occur for a social movement to develop?
a.   There must be a preexisting communication network.
b.   There must be a perceived sense of grievance among the potential participants in the movement or a strong desire for change.
c.   Since social movements are fueled by the news media, it is critical to utilize them to bring public attention to the movement's cause.
d.   All of the above

26. _____ is the process by which social movements and their leaders secure people and resources for the movement.
a.   Transformation
b.   Mobilization
c.   Acquisition
d.   Arm-twisting

27. The explanation of how social movements develop that focuses on how they gain momentum by successfully garnering resources, competing with pother movements, and mobilizing the resources available to them is
_____.
a.   political process theory
b.   new social movement theory
c.   resource mobilization theory
d.   functionalism

28. _____ theory posits that movements achieve success by exploiting a combination of internal factors, such as the ability of organizations to mobilize resources, and external factors, such as changes occurring in the society.
a.   Political process theory
b.   New social movement theory
c.   Resource mobilization theory
d.   Functionalism

29. _____ theory conceptually links culture, ideology, and identity to explain how new identities are forged within social movements.
a.   Individual conversion
b.   Personal conversion
c.   Personal transformation
d.   Human renovation

118

30. The increased interconnectedness and interdependence of different societies around the world is:
    a. gemeinschaft
    b. gesellschaft
    c. the world system
    d. globalization

True-False Statements.

1. According to Durkheim, social cohesiveness based on differences, such as division of labor which joins members of a society together because each depends on the others to perform specialized tasks is a characteristic of a gemeinschaft society.

2. Racial and ethnic conflict in the United States involves far more than class differences alone, since many cultural differences exist between Whites and Native Americans, African Americans, Latinos, and Asians.

3. The stage of social development where society struggles with the tension between the ideal and the practical is known as ideational culture.

4. The theory that all nations are part of a worldwide system of unequal political and economic relationships is modernization theory.

5. Modernization is typically characterized by a decline in small, traditional communities, increased bureaucratization, and an increase in the importance of the religious institution.

6. The United States since the 1940s has become a gesellschaft.

7. According to Riesman, persons who evidence strong conformity to long-standing and time-honored norms, practices, and styles of life are evidencing inner-directedness.

8. Extensive research over the past three decades demonstrate that elements of culture carried from Africa by Black slaves continue to survive among African Americans and among many other groups as well.

9. Immigration is having profound effects on the overall ethnic and racial composition of the U.S.

10. Forms of collective behavior, such as fads, crazes, and fashions, can initiate social change and may produce more sustained efforts at change, such as in the development of social movements.

11. Religious and cult movements are examples of reactionary social movements.

12. Radical movements seek change through legal or other mainstream political means, typically working within existing institutions.

13. While resource mobilization theory emphasizes the rational basis for social movement organization, new social movement theories are especially interested in how identity is socially constructed through participation in social movements.

14. Diversity results in unequal outcomes of change for different groups.

15. According to world systems theory, countries in Africa, Latin America, South America, and parts of Asia, which export raw materials and cheap labor to other nations, are known as core nations.

Short-Answer Questions.
A page reference to the relevant text material is provided in the parenthesis.

1. List and discuss the four characteristics of social change which were discussed in the textbook (416).

2. Compare and contrast the six major sociological theories of social change: functionalism and social evolution theory, conflict theory, cyclical theory, modernization theory, world systems theory, and dependency theory. Include in your discussion what each theory identifies as the primary cause of social change (417).

3. List and define the three principal personality orientations, according to David Riesman. Discuss the influence of social structural conditions on each of these personalities (424).

4. Define and describe each of the following types of social movements: personal transformation, social change, reform, and radical (431).

5. Compare and contrast the three theories of social movements discussed in the textbook: resource mobilization, political process, and new social movement theory (434).

ANSWERS TO THE MULTIPLE-CHOICE QUESTIONS.

1. B 415 The alterations of social interactions, institutions, stratification systems, and elements of culture over time is social change.

2. A 415 Gradual transformations that occur on a broad scale and affect many aspects of society are macrochanges.

3. D 416 Social change is uneven, since different parts of a society do not change at the same rate. Social change often creates conflict. The onset and consequences of social change are often unforeseen.

4. C 417 According to Durkheim, cohesion based on similarity among members in a society creates mechanical solidarity.

5. B 417 According to functionalist theorists, societies move from structurally simple, homogeneous societies, such as foraging or pastoral societies, to structurally more complex, heterogeneous societies, such as agricultural, industrial, and postindustrial societies.

6. B 418 The theory that argues that structural, institutional, and cultural development of a society can follow many evolutionary paths simultaneously, with the different paths all emerging from the circumstances of the society in question is multidimensional.

7. D 420 Cyclical theories of social change invoke patterns of social structure and culture that are believed to reoccur at more or less regular intervals.

8. A 420 According to Sorokin and Caplow, societies which stress practical approaches to reality and include hedonistic and sensual components are in the third phase of development which is known as the sensate.

9. C 421 The theory that states that global development is a worldwide process affecting nearly all societies that have been touched by technological change is modernization theory.

10. A 421. According to Wallerstein, world systems theory argues that all nations are members of a world wide system of unequal political and economic relationships, which benefits the developed and technologically advanced countries at the expense of the less technologically advanced and less developed countries.

11. D 421 Dependency theory maintains that highly industrialized nations tend to imprison developing nations in dependent relationships rather than spurring the higher mobility of developing countries with transfers of technology and business acumen.

12. B 422 The process of social and cultural change that is initiated by industrialization and followed by increased social differentiation and division of labor is modernization.

13. C 422 According to Tonnies, a society characterized by a sense of fellowship, strong personal ties, sturdy primary group memberships, and personal loyalty among group members is a gemeinschaft society.

14. B 423 According to Dahrendorf and Berger, modernization has produced a mass society, in which industrialization and bureaucracies reach exceedingly high levels.

15. B 424 A personality orientation in which the individual is guided by internal principles and morals and is relatively impervious to the superficialities of those around him or her is inner-directed.

16.	A	425	Cultural diffusion is the transmission of cultural elements from one society or cultural group to another.
17.	D	425	All of the following factors can influence social change: demographic changes, war, and technological innovations.
18.	B	427	Collective behavior occurs when normal conventions cease to guide proper behavior and people establish new patterns of interaction and social structure.
19.	C	428	Communication between persons and communication between persons and computers is known as cyberspace.
20.	D	429	Collective behavior may emerge spontaneously in response to a unique situation, is innovative and sometimes revolutionary, and may include crowds, riots, disasters, fads, fashions, and social movements.
21.	A	431	Reactionary movements, such as the White supremacy movement and the large number of hate groups in the United States, are attempts to resist change toward greater racial equality.
22.	C	431	Personal transformation movements focus on the development of new meaning within individual lives rather than pursuing social change.
23.	A	432	Social movements, such as the environmental movement, that gay and lesbian movement, the civil rights movement, the animal rights movement, and the religious right movement, are examples of social change movements.
24.	D	432	Those movements that seek change through legal or other mainstream political means and typically work within existing institutions are reform movements.
25.	D	432	Social movements do not typically develop out of thin air. There must be a preexisting communication network. There must be a perceived sense of grievance among the potential participants in the movement or a strong desire for change. Since social movements are fueled by the news media, it is critical to utilize them to bring public attention to the movement's cause.
26.	B	433	Mobilization is the process by which social movements and their leaders secure people and resources for the movement.
27.	C	434	The explanation of how social movements develop that focuses on how they gain momentum by successfully garnering resources, competing with pother movements, and mobilizing the resources available to them is resource mobilization theory.
28.	A	434	Political process theory posits that movements achieve success by exploiting a combination of internal factors, such as the ability of organizations to mobilize resources, and external factors, such as changes occurring in the society.
29.	B	434	Personal conversion theory conceptually links culture, ideology, and identity to explain how new identities are forged within social movements.
30.	D	435	The increased interconnectedness and interdependence of different societies around the world is globalization.

ANSWERS TO THE TRUE-FALSE STATEMENTS.

1.	F	417	According to Durkheim, social cohesiveness based on differences, such as division of labor which joins members of a society together because each depends on the others to perform specialized tasks is a characteristic of a gesellschaft society.
2.	T	419	Racial and ethnic conflict in the United States involves far more than class differences alone, since many cultural differences exist between Whites and Native Americans, African Americans, Latinos, and Asians.
3.	F	420	The stage of social development where society struggles with the tension between the ideal and the practical is known as idealistic culture.
4.	F	421	The theory that all nations are part of a worldwide system of unequal political and economic relationships is world systems theory.
5.	F	422	Modernization is typically characterized by a decline in small, traditional communities, increased bureaucratization, and an decline in the importance of the religious institution.
6.	T	423	The United States since the 1940s has become a gesellschaft.
7.	F	424	According to Riesman, persons who evidence strong conformity to long-standing and time-honored norms, practices, and styles of life are evidencing tradition-directedness.

8.   T   426   Extensive research over the past three decades demonstrate that elements of culture carried from Africa by Black slaves continue to survive among African Americans and among many other groups as well.

9.   T   427   Immigration is having profound effects on the overall ethnic and racial composition of the U.S.

10.   T   427   Forms of collective behavior, such as fads, crazes, and fashions, can initiate social change and may produce more sustained efforts at change, such as in the development of social movements.

11.   F   431   Religious and cult movements are examples of personal transformation social movements.

12.   F   432   Reform movements seek change through legal or other mainstream political means, typically working within existing institutions.

13.   T   434   While resource mobilization theory emphasizes the rational basis for social movement organization, new social movement theories are especially interested in how identity is socially constructed through participation in social movements.

14.   T   436   Diversity results in unequal outcomes of change for different groups.

15.   F   421   According to world systems theory, countries in Africa, Latin America, South America, and parts of Asia, which export raw materials and cheap labor to other nations, are known as noncore or peripheral nations.